THE LATEST S. GALAXY S24 ULTRA USER MANUAL

A guide full of impressive features capable of give users remarkable experience ever

Serah Paul

Table of Contents

INTRODUCTION

The 24MP camera on the Samsung Galaxy S24 UItra is impressive. The typical camera resolution is 24MP. It is thought to be an improvement over the Galaxy S23 model, including a 12MP camera. It is also discovered that the super smartphone has a photo remaster feature. With the AI-powered features of the Samsung Galaxy S24 UItra, users may eliminate shadows from their images.

The Samsung Galaxy S24 UItra has three settings: erase, portrait, and remaster. One of its characteristics is the neutral density filter, or ND filter. This feature allows users of the Samsung Galaxy S24 UItra to change the colors and brightness levels of original photos.

The AI features of S24 Ultra will also help customers record high-quality video clips and capture the entire zoomed-in area. High definition footage is recorded for the videos.

Because tracking characteristics and the capacity to capture moving objects take care of things, users no longer need to make manual modifications. In this regard, shooting video with the Samsung Galaxy S24 Ultra will be smooth, knowledgeable, and improved.

The Samsung Galaxy S24 Ultra boasts a quad back 200 MP camera with AI assistance. This smartphone's camera features a 12MP ultra wide-angle sensor, a 50MP sensor, a 10MP sensor, and a 5X telephoto lens. The rear camera on this model has features like optical image stabilization (OIS) and can record 8K films.

Powering this upscale smartphone is the Qualcomm Snapdragon 8 Gen 3 SoC, which features GPU cores and an overclocked GPU.

The Snapdragon 3 chipset that the Samsung Galaxy S24 Ultra smartphone will come with has been revealed; this will affect the device's performance.

The latest Samsung Exynos chipsets will be included in the launching of the Ultra version. Its excellent performance is advantageous to users. The standard Galaxy S24 and S24 plus will receive an Exynos chipset update along with the debut of the Samsung Galaxy S24 UItra smartphone.

The Samsung Galaxy S24 UItra smartphone has 8GB RAM and 128GB of internal storage. The device is running the Android operating system. It features GPS, Bluetooth, and USB Type-C. It is powered by a Li-Po 5100mAh battery and a 6.8-inch dynamic AMOLED display with a pixel resolution of 1440 x 3200. This smartphone boasts a quad camera configuration with 50 MP (telephoto) + 200 MP (wide) + 10 MP + 12 MP (ultrawide). Additionally, it has two SIM card slots. A 32MP front camera is present. One advantage of the Samsung Galaxy S24 UItra is its array of sensors, which includes a barometer, proximity, gyro, accelerometer, compass, and display fingerprint.

Galaxy S24 Ultra

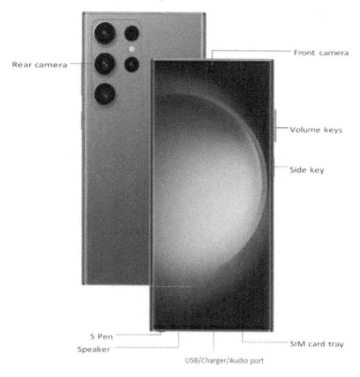

Rear camera

Front camera

Volume keys

Side key

S Pen

Speaker

USB/Charger/Audio port

SIM card tray

Galaxy S24+

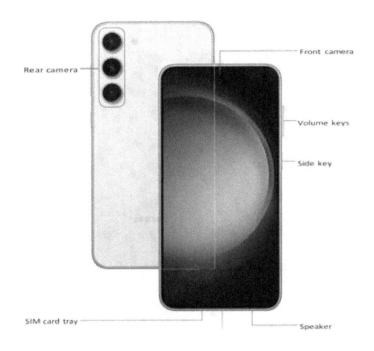

The Galaxy S24+ utilizes a nano-SIM card. You can either buy a pre-loaded card or use your old SIM card. The 5G network indicators provided by your service provider are based on the availability and specifications of the network.

The Galaxy S24+ is IP68-rated, which means it can withstand water and dust. To ensure that its features are protected, make sure that your device's SIM card tray is free of dust and water. Also, ensure that the tray is secure in place before being exposed to liquids.

Maintaining water and dust resistance

Keep in mind that this device should not be charged while it's wet to avoid getting damaged or electric shock. Also, avoid using the device and charging cords with wet hands.

The device can't be considered resilient to water and dust damage. It's important to keep all of its compartments closed tightly.

Follow these steps to protect and maintain the device's water and dust resistance. IP68-rated devices are able to withstand submersion in water up to 1.5 meters deep. If you're worried about damaging the device, make sure that it's thoroughly dry before using it. After washing the device, use a soft cloth to remove any dirt and grime.

It is essential to ensure that any device with access ports and compartments that are accessible must have these closed and sealed to prevent the entry of fluids into the system.

If the device is submerged in water or the speaker is wet, the sound quality may not be as clear as it should be during a call. To prevent this issue, make sure that the device is thoroughly dry before you use it.

The device's dust and water-resistant features could be damaged if it gets hit or dropped. Foreign or dust particles could also enter the receiver, speaker, or microphone.

Some functions may not work or the sound may become quiet. If you're trying to remove foreign materials or dust with a sharp object, it might damage the device and its appearance.

An air vent hole may become covered by an accessory, which could result in unwanted noises during media playback or calls.

Keep in mind that liquids other than water can enter the device at a faster rate than fresh water. Failure to thoroughly clean the device could cause it to have cosmetic or operability issues.

CHAPTER ONE

Charge the battery

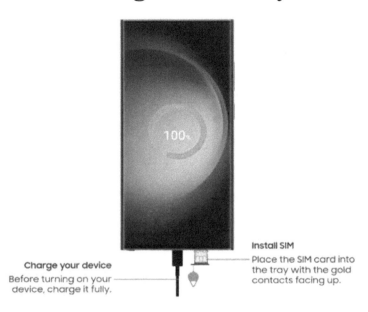

Charge your device
Before turning on your device, charge it fully.

Install SIM
Place the SIM card into the tray with the gold contacts facing up.

A rechargeable battery powers up your device.

Always use the Samsung-approved charging cables and chargers for your device. In order to prevent damage or injury, avoid using devices with mismatched or worn batteries or other incompatible accessories. Also, using other devices that have not been certified by Samsung may lead to issues.

When the charging cable and the device become too hot, it may prevent the device from fully charging. This issue usually doesn't affect the device's performance or lifespan. If this occurs, you can try unplugging the charger and waiting for the device to cool itself down.

Wireless power sharing

You can wirelessly power up your Samsung Galaxy devices using your phone. However, some of the features are not supported while using power sharing.

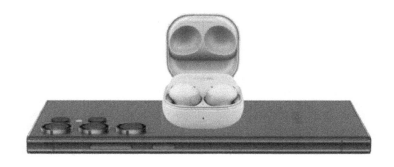

In order to use wireless power sharing, go to Settings and select Battery and Device Care. Then, choose the percentage of the battery that you want to use. When the device has reached its charging capacity, power sharing will automatically stop. You can also turn on the feature by placing the compatible device on top of the Galaxy S24 Ultra to charge.

Most Qi-Certified devices work with wireless power sharing. However, you should be aware that the speed and efficiency of the charge vary depending on the model and its battery. In addition, you may not be able to use it with certain accessories or covers.

Please note that the wireless power sharing feature is best used with devices that have a Qi-Certified chipset.

Before using wireless power sharing, make sure that you remove any accessories that are not compatible with the device. This can prevent the feature from working properly.

The placement of the charging coil may vary depending on the device. In order to provide you with an indication of successful connection, a vibration or notification will be displayed once the power sharing feature starts.

Data and call services may experience issues when using wireless power sharing. The efficiency or speed of the charge may vary depending on the environment. Also, refrain from using headphones while using wireless power sharing.

CHAPTER TWO

Set up your device

The device should be turned on using the Side key. Don't use it if the device is broken or cracked. It should only be used after the repairs have been completed.

To turn the device on, press and hold the Side key.

To turn off the device, press and hold the Volume down and Side keys at the same time. Then, tap on the Power off button.

Hold the Volume down and Side keys simultaneously and press the restart button. Confirm the prompt.

From the Settings app, go to Advanced and select the Side key and then choose How to power your device off.

Navigate to the Advanced features section and select the Side key option, and then choose How to Power Your Phone Off.

The optimal 5G experience requires a fast and reliable connection with an unobstructed antenna on the rear of the device. Issues related to cases or covers may also affect the performance of this feature.

Use the Setup Wizard

The first time you turn on your device, the wizard will guide you through the steps in setting up your device.

You'll be prompted to follow the steps to configure your device and connect to a Wi-Fi network. You can also set up accounts, locate services, and learn more about its features.

Bring data from an old device

You can easily transfer photos, music, messages, notes, calendar entries, and contacts from your old device with the help of Smart Switch. It can be done through a computer, a USB cable, or Wi-Fi.

To learn more about the features of Smart Switch, please visit the company's website at samsung.com/smartswitch.

After navigating to the settings, select the option to bring data from your old device and follow the prompts.

The lock screen and security features are available on your device. They can be used to protect your device whenever the screen is not active. More information about these features can be found in the app or in the security section.

The images presented are for illustrative purposes only and do not reflect the current state of the art of software and devices.

Side key settings

Customize the shortcuts that are assigned to the Side key. You can also choose which features are launched whenever the key is pressed twice. To do so, go to the Advanced features section and tap on the Side key option.

Side key
Press to lock.
Press to turn on the
screen, and then
swipe the screen to
unlock it.

Double-press the option to enable the Quick Launch camera and then choose the option to open the app.

Press and hold

Hold and press the Side key to choose which feature will be launched next. From the Settings app, go to the Advanced features section and select the Side key option. On the next page, tap on the option that says "Wake

Bixby." You can also set up accounts and manage your contacts, calendar, and email accounts.

Add a Google Account

To access your Google Cloud storage and other installed apps, sign in to your Google Account. You can also use the device's various Android features.

After you've set up a lock screen and signed in to a Google account, Google Device Protection will automatically activate. This feature requires your Google account details when you reset to factory settings.

Go to the Settings app and select the option to manage your contacts, backup, and accounts. You can also add a Samsung account to your Google account.

Add a Samsung account

To add a Samsung account to your Outlook email, go to the Settings app and choose the option that says "Add account." In the next section, click on the option that says "Manage accounts." You can also set up voicemail.

First-time users can set up voicemail using the Phone app. The options for different service providers may vary.

To set up voicemail, tap the option from the Phone app and hold the 1 key. Follow the instructions to create a greeting, record your name, and create a password.

CHAPTER THREE

Navigation

The optimal way to use a touch screen is by gently swiping your finger across the pad of your stylus or finger. Excessive force or the presence of a metallic object on the screen may bend or damage its surface, and this issue won't be covered by the manufacturer's warranty.

Tap

To launch or select an item, tap lightly on it. To zoom in or out, double-tap an image, and then gently drag your finger across it.

To use the device, swipe the screen to

either unlock it or navigate through the various home screen or menu options.

To use the device, swipe the screen to either unlock it or navigate through the various home screen or menu options.

Swipe

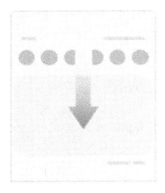

Drag and drop an item and move it to a different location. Drag a shortcut that will add it to the home screen or a widget that will place it in a different location. To zoom in and out, hold your forefinger and thumb together or apart.

Darg and drop

To zoom in or move your forefinger and thumb apart, respectively, to zoom in and out.

Touch and hold

Hold the field to show a pop-up menu or touch and hold the home screen to customize it.

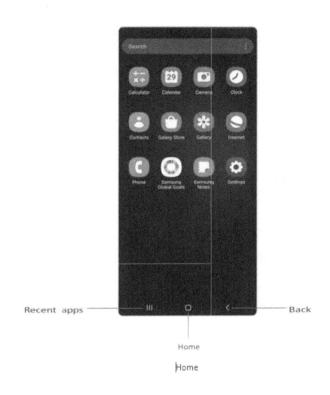

Recent apps   III   O   <   Back

Home

Home

Navigation bar

You can use gestures or the navigation buttons to navigate the device. The home button is located at the bottom of the screen, and it allows users to quickly access the various features of the device.

Under the Button order, choose which part of the Home screen the Recent apps and Back icons will appear on.

Navigation gestures

To prevent clutter and enhance the overall experience, remove the navigation buttons from the bottom of the screen. Instead, swipe to navigate.

To enable the feature, go to the Settings app, select the navigation bar, and then swipe gestures. You can also customize the appearance of the screen by choosing a gesture type and setting up display lines at the bottom.

When gesture hints are disabled, you can only switch apps using them while they're hidden. You can also hide the keyboard by showing an icon in the bottom right corner, which will hide it when the device is turned on in portrait mode.

Customize your home screen

The home screen is where you can place your apps and other content. You can also customize it by adding new home screens, removing them, and choosing a primary one.

The home screen displays app icons to add an app. To do so, tap on the icon and then select "Add to Home." To remove an icon, hold the icon and then tap "Remove." Note that this method does not remove the app, but it takes it away from the home screen.

You can personalize the look of the home and lock screens by choosing a preferred image, video, or pre-loaded wallpaper.

First, you can access the home screen by touching and holding it. You can then tap on the style and the selection of wallpapers. You can also select the lock screen and home screen images to modify them. You can additionally download or choose from a wide range of options and themes.

The Color Palette can be customized based on the colors in your wallpapers. You can also enable the Dark mode feature to change the wallpaper's appearance. You can additionally customize the look of the home and lock screens by setting a theme.

You can select the colors of your wallpapers using the color palette. You can also set a theme that will be used on your home and lock screens, as well as app icons and wallpapers. To download or preview a theme, go to the Themes section and tap on it.

Go to the Themes section and choose the one that you want to use on your home and lock screens. You can also download and preview a theme by choosing an icon set. To replace the default icons, tap on the different icon sets.

You can view and apply the icons that you've downloaded by going to the My stuff > Icons section and selecting the appropriate icon set. You can add various widget sets to your home screens so that you can easily access apps and information.

Go to the home screen and select the widget that you want to add. You can then customize its appearance and function by pressing and holding on it. You can also create a stack of similar sized items by adding them to the same screen.

You can remove a widget from your device. You can also customize its appearance and function through the settings. In addition, you can review the app usage and permissions of the widget.

You can configure your device to have one home screen that's exclusively for apps and separate from the others.

To view and apply the downloaded icons, go to the My stuff > icons section. After selecting the appropriate icon set, tap the Apply button. You can use these to add various widget sets that will allow you to access apps and information quickly.

Tap the Add button to add the widget you want to use. You can then customize how it functions and where it's located. You can also create stack objects, which are similar in size, by adding them to the same area on the home screen.

You may remove a widget from the home screen. Through the settings, you can modify its appearance or function. You can also review the app permissions, usage, and more. Navigate to your home screen and tap on the settings to customize it.

You can configure your device to either have one home screen with a dedicated app for apps or one with all the apps in one place.

The home screen layout that you prefer will determine the arrangement of the icons. On the other hand, the apps and folders grid will let you know how they are organized.

You can add a media page to the home screen by swiping right from the home screen. You can then view the various media services that are available.

You can show the apps screen with a button on the home screen. This allows you to easily access the various apps that are available on your device.

The lock screen layout blocks the items from moving around or being removed. It also adds new apps automatically.

To hide apps from the home and app screens, select the ones that you want to hide. To remove them, go to the "hidden" category and then return to the main screen. These apps remain installed and can be found as part of the Finder searches.

You can show app icon badges with notifications enabled. You can also customize the style of the badge.

You can swipe down on the notification panel to enable this feature and open it from anywhere on the home screen.

You can also automatically rotate the home screen whenever the device's orientation changes from portrait to landscape.

The home screen of your device displays the latest version and information. You can also contact Samsung through its members for help.

Easy mode

The Easy mode layout utilizes larger icons and text for a more organized and visually appealing experience. You can switch between the default and simpler layouts when needed.

To enable this feature, go to the home screen and tap on the option that you want to enable.

One of the options that you can enable is the delay in the recognition of touch and hold. This allows you to set the time it takes for the continuous touch to be considered a hold and touch.

You can select a keyboard with vibrant colors by going to the settings and choosing High contrast.

The products and software of Samsung are constantly evolving, so the illustrations presented here are for reference only.

Status bar

The status bar provides various information about the device, such as its battery level and location. It also displays notifications on the left side. Some of these include a call in progress, an alarm, and a new message.

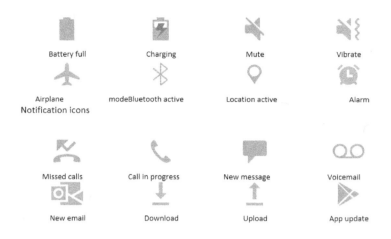

Battery full	Charging	Mute	Vibrate
Airplane	modeBluetooth active	Location active	Alarm

Notification icons

Missed calls	Call in progress	New message	Voicemail
New email	Download	Upload	App update

To configure the status bar for notifications, go to the Quick settings and select More options.

Notification panel

The Notification panel is a convenient tool that lets you quickly access various settings and notifications. It can be used from any screen. You can swipe down to show the panel and open an item, or drag the notification to either the right or left side to remove it.

The software and devices of Samsung are constantly evolving, so the illustrations presented here are for reference only.

To remove all of the notifications, go to your device's settings and select Clear. To customize them, tap on the notification settings. Drag the notification up or down from the bottom or close it by tapping Back.

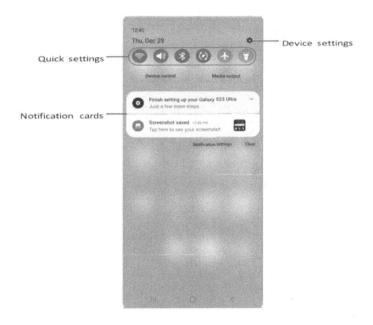

The Quick settings provide users with quick access to their device's functions. The icons shown below highlight the most frequently used Quick settings. Their colors will change once enabled or disabled. Other options may be available on the device.

Go to the Notification panel and drag the status bar down to show the panel. Then, swipe down from the top of the device to access the Quick settings. You can also turn on or off the setting by holding the icon. Wi-Fi Direct, Airplane mode, and Power saving Dark mode are some of the options that are available in the Quick settings.

The navigation bar will take you to the device's search facility. You can also access the device's settings menu. There are more options that allow users to customize the layout of the buttons or revert to the Quick settings.

When you have supported apps such as Google Home and SmartThings installed, you can control other devices.

The Media output panel allows users to control the playback of content from their connected devices. Brightness slider can also be used to adjust the overall screen brightness.

CHAPTER FOUR

S Pen

The S Pen has various useful features, such as launching apps, taking notes, and drawing a picture. Some of these may not work if the Galaxy S24 Ultra is near a magnet.

The S Pen has a variety of useful features, such as launching apps, taking notes, and drawing pictures. Some of these may not work if your device is located near a magnet.

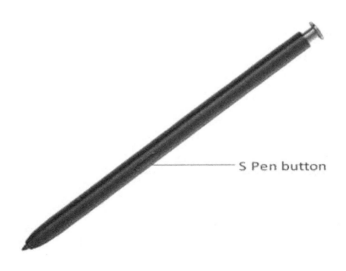

S Pen button

Remove the S Pen

The S Pen can be found in the bottom of your device, and it charges to allow users to use it remotely.

To remove the S Pen, press the stylus inward and slide it out.

To ensure that your device's water-resistant features are protected, make sure that the opening and slot for the S Pen are clean and free of dust and water. The stylus should also be securely inserted before being exposed to liquids.

The images presented here are for illustrative purposes only and do not reflect the current state of software and devices.

Air view

The Air view feature allows users to preview content and view details about an item while hovering over the screen.

Users can preview an email message and examine the contents of an image or a photo album. They can also preview videos and navigate to specific scenes by hovering over a timeline. The ability to preview content is only available if the stylus has a solid color.

With the S Pen, users can perform remote tasks using their gestures or button. It can also create shortcuts for their favorite apps, navigate the screens of their devices, and complete actions.

Only the S Pen with Bluetooth Low Energy support is supported by the remote feature. If the device is too far from the stylus, it will disconnect from the gadget. Users must also have the device connected to use the Air actions feature.

Only Samsung-approved S Pens equipped with Bluetooth Low Energy support will work with the remote feature. It will disconnect from the device if it's too far away or if it gets interfered with.

Air Actions

Users can use the stylus with the gesture or button to perform remote tasks. It can create shortcuts for their preferred apps, browse the screens of their gadgets, and perform other tasks.

The BLE-equipped S Pen works only with Samsung-approved devices. If the stylus is too far away or if there's interference, it will disconnect from the gadget. The Air actions feature requires a tethered device to use.

To enable the Air actions feature, go to the Advanced features section and select the S Pen option.

Hold the S Pen button shortcut

You can set a shortcut for the S Pen by pressing and holding it. This shortcut will automatically launch the Camera app.

Tap the Advanced features option from the Settings menu. Then, select the Air actions category.

Anywhere actions

The Anywhere actions feature allows users to customize their devices' shortcuts by pressing and holding the S Pen. These shortcuts can be accessed by making various gestures, such as shaking or up, and can be used to access various features and apps.

To use the Action Gesture, go to the home screen, select the menu option, and then select the Air actions category. You can also customize the shortcut by pressing and holding the icon. The stylus can be used to perform specific actions in specific apps.

To view Air actions and the available shortcuts, go to the Settings menu, then Advanced features, and select Air actions. Then, enable the shortcuts in the app that you're using.

General app actions

While using media and camera apps that aren't in the app action list, users can customize their general actions.

Back		Left to right
Recents		Right to left
Home		Up and down
Smart select		Down and up
Screen write		Zigzag

Go to the Settings menu and select Advanced features and S Pen. Then, choose Air actions.

Screen off memo

Although you can write memos using the stylus without turning on the device, you must have enabled ⬤ the screen off mode to use it.

After enabling the screen off mode, remove the S Pen and write using it. You can also change the pen's color or tap on its settings to adjust the thickness of the line. Lastly, you can use the eraser tool to remove all or just a portion of the memo. You can save the entire work by going to the Notes app and choosing Save Memo.

If the S Pen has been removed from your device, press the button and then tap on the screen to start a note.

Pin to Always On Display

You can also pin or change a memo on the Always On display. To do so, go to the screen off memo and tap on the Pin 📌 to Always On display option.

Air command

You can use the signature features of the S Pen on different screens with the ability to access Screen write, Smart select, and Samsung Notes.

Settings

Hold the ⬤ S Pen at the screen and wait for the pointer to appear before pressing the button once.

To create a new note, go to the Samsung Notes app and ⊕ choose the option to create. You can also view and 🗐 organize all of your notes by launching the app and looking for the notes that you've created.

The illustrations presented here are for reference only and are not indicative of the current state of affairs of the device or software.

You can use Smart select to draw around the screen to find the area you want in the Gallery. You can also capture screenshots and doodle using the S Pen. You can create live messages and interactive doodles with the help of the AR camera.

Hover the S Pen over a certain word and it will translate it into another language, and you can listen to its pronunciation.

You can use the S Pen to create and color illustrations, as well as share them. You can also add more apps and functions to the Air menu through the Add button.

You can customize the Air command by adding apps and functions and changing the menu's appearance.

Create note

You can launch a ⬤ new note within the Samsung Notes

app ⬤, and it will be available for viewing later. You can

also open the app and view all of your notes, ⬤ as well

as a listing of the ones that you have created.

Smart select

Sharing content from any screen is possible with the

Smart select feature. ⬤ You can drag and drop it into

your Gallery app or send it to your contacts.

Smart select lets you copy and paste content from

different screens. You can either send it to your

contacts or add it to the Gallery app.

Go to the Air menu and choose Smart select. Drag

and drop the S Pen to the content that you want to

extract. There are several options that you can choose

from, such as inserting or placing shortcuts on your home

screen or in an app. ⬤ Auto select will let Smart select

automatically extract content.

Captured content can be drawn using Smart select. Text can be extracted from the selected area using the extraction tool. You can also choose to share the content using the sharing method.

Tap the Animation option to create an animated video or pin to the screen for Smart select.

Screen write

You can capture and draw on screenshots with the Screen write feature. You can use the pen tool to take screenshots or doodle on them after the current screen has been captured. There are various editing tools that you can use to enhance the captured content, such as the Crop option.

You can use the Pen to draw on a screenshot. You can change its size, color, and tip by tapping the icon twice.

The eraser will remove the drawings or writing on the screenshot. Undoing will undo the last undone action. The next one is called "Redo." The mode that you prefer to use for sharing your content is "Share." You can also capture any area of the screen that's hidden, and the content will be saved to the Gallery app.

To remove your pen drawings on the screen, hold the S Pen button. You can then use the Live messages feature to record an animated message or a written one. To choose the background for the message, tap Air > Live messages.

The Gallery app displays all of the live messages that you've created. You can also choose the background image or video that you want to use for the message.

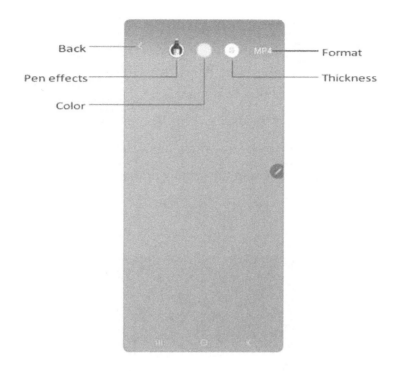

Back
Pen effects
Color

Format
Thickness

Pick the color for the background. Follow the prompts to begin the live message creation process. You can then tap Done to save.

These illustrations are only meant to be used for reference. You should keep in mind that the devices and software used are constantly changing.

AR Doodle

You can doodle on various objects captured using augmented reality. You can start by using the Air command to set up the camera. You can also tap on the Switch camera to choose which one you want to focus on. Position the camera in the middle of the screen so that it's in the center. Lastly, use the S Pen to create a doodle.

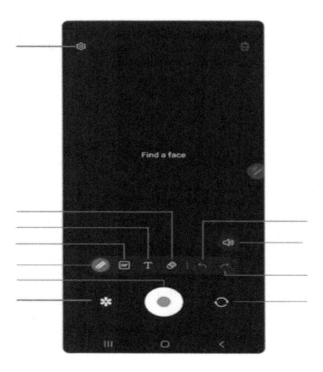

The doodle uses real-time movement data to create a representation of the face. You can then save the video of your AR doodle by pressing Record.

The software and devices used are constantly evolving. Therefore, the illustrations presented here are only meant for reference.

Translate

With the S Pen, you can easily translate and listen to the pronunciation of words by hovering over them. You can also change the icon that appears when translating a phrase or a word. You can also change the languages that you want to target by tapping the target and source languages.

To listen to the word's pronunciation in the source language, use the Sound feature. Then, tap Copy to save the translated text and close Translate. You can use the S Pen for various other tasks such as drawing, color, and sharing live illustrations.

To customize the Air menu, tap the Pen > PENUP option. You can add shortcuts to the menu. You can also choose the apps and functions that you want to use by pressing the Add button. To remove ⊕ a shortcut, tap the Remove button. Tap the Save option to save your selection.

The Pen and apps menus are collapsible so that you can easily access them from anywhere on the screen.

The collapsible and convenient menus allow you to quickly access the various features of the Pen and apps.

To configure the Air menu, go to the Settings app and select Advanced features. Then, choose the style of the menu that you want to see when the menu is opened.

You can select the Air command's shortcuts and show or hide the icon for the menu.

The Air command can be opened using the S Pen button.

Configure S Pen settings

The S Pen's settings can be customized. Service providers may have different options.

To configure the S Pen's features, go to the Settings app and select Advanced features. Then, you can configure the Air actions that allow you to control the device using apps.

The Air command menu can be customized with the settings for the shortcuts, behavior, and appearance. The Air view can be turned on or off.

S Pen users can write in various text areas, such as search fields and address bars, with the help of the pen. It converts handwriting into text and allows users to edit it with the help of the pen.

When the S Pen is removed, you can select what happens after detaching it. You can do nothing, open the Air command, or create a note.

When the screen is turned off, users can detach the S Pen and then write using it on the screen while it's off. Memos created using this method are saved in Samsung Notes app.

Hold the S Pen button and then tap the screen multiple times to open a new note.

You can configure the S Pen to behave differently, such as vibrating, connecting, and sounds.

You can view the latest version of the S Pen and its associated software through the official Samsung site. You can also contact the company's support center through its members.

Bixby

Samsung's virtual assistant, Bixby, is designed to evolve and adapt to you. It can learn your routines and provide you with personalized reminders based on your location and time. You can also use it in your favorite apps.

Press and hold the Side key to access Bixby. You can also access it through the apps list.

Bixby Vision

Through its integration with your gallery, Internet, and camera apps, Bixby can provide you with a deeper understanding of your surroundings. It can also perform various functions such as searching for and recording QR codes, reading quotes, and shopping.

Camera

On the camera's viewfinder, tap on the Bixby Vision icon and follow the prompts to learn more about the image you're viewing.

Gallery

Bixby Vision can be used on images and pictures that have been saved in the Gallery app. To use it, tap on a picture and follow the prompts.

Internet

In the Internet app, ⬤ hold and touch the image to get a pop-up menu with the Bixby Vision icon. Follow the prompts to search for and learn more about the image.

Modes and Routines

You can customize your device's settings by setting up routines and ⬤ modes that will automatically adjust them based on your specific situation or activity.

To navigate through the various options, go to the Settings app and click on the "Modes" and "Routines" buttons. The former allows you to choose a mode based on your location and activities. On the other hand, the latter lets you create routines that are specific to your surroundings.

Parental controls and digital wellbeing are among the options that you can configure. You can also customize your settings by setting up routines and modes that will automatically adjust them based on your specific situation or activity.

Digital wellbeing and parental controls

You can monitor and control your digital behavior by getting a daily summary of your activities, such as how many notifications you get, how often you open apps, and how much time you spend checking your device. You may also set it to help you fall asleep before you get up.

To view the various features of the app, go to the settings and click on the Digital Wellbeing and Parental controls. You can view the time spent using and opened an app, as well as the number of notifications sent out each day. You can also see the number of times an app was opened or unlocked.

You can set a goal for your screen time and set a daily limit on how long you can use each app.

You can monitor your device's screen time and the apps that you're using while you're driving using the Bluetooth connection of your car.

You can select a source to determine the volume and ensure your ears are protected with this choice.

Google's Family Link app is a parental control tool that helps supervise the digital life of your kids. It allows you to filter content and limit the time they spend on their device.

Always On Display

You can check the status of missed calls and messages, view customized information, and look up the time and date with the help of Always On Display.

To enable the feature, go to the settings, and then select Always On Display. You can also set the time when the notifications and clock will appear on the screen while your device is not being used.

You can change the appearance and colors of the clock on the lock screen and Always On Display.

The music control of Face Widgets will show the details of the playlist when the device is used.

When the Face Widgets Music Controller is enabled, the music details of the playlist will be shown on the screen. In landscape or portrait mode, the AOD can be displayed. You can also set the automatic brightness of the feature to adjust. You can additionally check the current version of the software and license information.

AOD themes

You can customize your device with custom themes that are available for Always On Display. To download and preview these themes, go to your home screen and tap on the "Themes" button. You can then tap on the "Apply" button to complete the process. You can also use biometric security to secure your device and log in to your accounts.

CHAPTER FIVE

Face recognition

Enabling face recognition will allow you to access the screen using your face. To use this feature, you must have a PIN, password, or pattern.

The lack of security of facial recognition compared to other methods is less secure. It could be used by someone to access your device, even if it looks like you are wearing a mask.

Some facial features can affect how facial recognition is performed. These include wearing makeup, wearing a hat, or having a beard.

Make sure that you are in an area that's well-lit, and the camera lens should be clean. To register your face, follow the prompts and set up facial recognition. You can also customize the way it works by going to the settings and choosing "Biometrics."

An alternative appearance can help enhance facial recognition.

Enable or disable facial recognition security.

When you enable facial recognition, you should always swipe through the lock screen before unlocking your device.

When you have open eyes, facial recognition will only be able to recognize your face.

To help your device recognize your face in low light conditions, try increasing the brightness of the screen.

Learn more about how to use facial recognition to safeguard your device.

Fingerprint scanner

With fingerprint authentication, you can log in to certain apps without entering a password.

Samsung allows users to verify their identity by using their fingerprint. Users need to set a password, PIN, or pattern to access their device.

To set up fingerprint authentication, go to your device's settings and choose "Biometrics." You can then follow the prompts to add, delete, or rename your fingerprint.

The list of fingerprints that are registered is the top one. You can rename or remove it.

You can add another fingerprint by following the prompts. You can then check whether it has been registered by scanning it.

Fingerprint verification settings

You can use your fingerprint to verify your identity in apps and actions supported by your device. From the settings, go to the Biometrics section and choose "Biometrics." You can then use your fingerprint to unlock your device.

When the screen is off, show the fingerprint icon. When you use fingerprint authentication, show an animation while you're unlocking.

Biometrics settings

You can configure your preferences when it comes to using biometric security. Under Privacy and Security, go to the section that says "Biometrics."

Transition effects can be displayed when you use biometric authentication to unlock your device.

You should know more about how to secure your device with biometric authentication.

Multi window

You can multitask using several applications at the same time using Multi window technology. Certain apps that support this feature can be mounted on a split-screen display. You can also change the size of the windows and switch between them.

Split screen control

Split screen control

To use the split screen control, tap the Recent apps icon from any screen. Then, tap the app icon in the other window to add an app to the view. You can also change the window's size by dragging the middle section.

These illustrations are only references and do not reflect the current state of the software and devices.

Window controls

The window controls modify how apps appear on a split-screen display. Drag the middle portion of the window border to change its size. You can also switch between the two windows by pressing the middle section. You can then add a shortcut for an app to the Edge panel.

Edge panels

The Edge panels, which are customizable, let users access various applications, contacts, and tasks from the edge of their device. They can also be used to check sports scores, look up news, and view other information.

To enable this feature, go to the Settings app and select Edge panels.

Edge panels

Go to the Settings app and select the Edge panels. On the left-hand side, choose "Apps." You can add applications to the panel.

Drag the Edge handle over the center of the screen and swipe to the right to reveal the apps panel.

To open an app or pair, tap the respective shortcut. You can also go to the complete list of applications to see all of them.

Drag the app icon from the apps panel to the open screen to open additional windows in the pop-up view.

The software and devices are constantly evolving, so the illustrations presented here are only for reference.

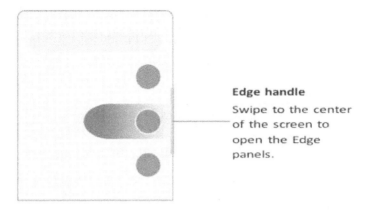

Edge handle
Swipe to the center of the screen to open the Edge panels.

To configure Apps panel:

Drag the Edge handle over the center of the screen and swipe to the right to reveal the apps panel.

Tap the Edit button to add new applications to the panel.

You can add a new app to the panel by finding it on the left-hand side of the screen and then tap on it to add it to the right-hand column.

Drag one app from the left-hand screen over another in the right-hand columns to create a shortcut for folders.

Drag one or all of the applications to the desired location to change the order of the panel's applications. You can also remove an app by pressing the Remove button.

Configure Edge panels

To customize the Edge panels, go to Settings > Edge panels. There are various options that you can select, such as enabling or disabling each panel. You can also customize individual panels or search for those that are already installed.

Drag the panels to the right or left to change their order. You can also uninstall or remove them from your device. To hide the Edge panels on the lock screen, select the option to hide them. You can find and download more panels from the Galaxy Store.

Go back to the settings and save the changes. You can change the way the Edge handle appears on the screen by dragging it along the edge. You can also set the orientation of the Edge screen to either the left or right side.

Enables the ability to prevent the Edge handle from being moved whenever touched or held.

The choice of a color can be selected for the Edge handle. You can also customize its transparency by dragging the slider. The slider for size can be used to adjust the Edge handle's width.

The license information and software version of the Edge panels are shown in the About Edge panels section of the Settings app. You can also enter text using your voice or keyboard.

Illustrations presented here are only for reference and should not be considered complete. The software and devices are constantly changing.

Toolbar

The keyboard's toolbar offers quick access to various features. The service provider's options may vary. To access the keyboard's features, tap on the Expand toolbar from the Samsung keyboard.

Expand toolbar

You can explore different emoji types, emojis, GIFs, and custom combinations. You can also use the clipboard to access it.

A one-handed keyboard can be used with a layout that's ideal for those who prefer to use their device with one hand. You can also type text using your handwriting using the Galaxy S23 Ultra's handwriting feature.

Changing the keyboard's appearance to a floating one that can be used anywhere on the screen is very convenient.

You can search for specific phrases or words in your conversations or translate sentences into another language. You can also extract text from the content of your chosen articles. Samsung Pass, which uses biometrics, allows users to quickly access their online accounts and personal data.

You can get Grammarly suggestions as you type, and various other emoji and GIF options are available. You can also customize your own emoji or use them in stickers with the help of Bitmoji, Mojitok, or AR Emoji. You can sync your music with Spotify.

You can add videos to YouTube. The keyboard's height and width can be adjusted. You can also use an editing panel to select text that you want to be copied, cut, or paste.

Configure the Samsung keyboard

You can configure the keyboard for Samsung devices with different options depending on the service provider.

You can set the keyboard's type and choose the languages that it supports.

To switch to another language, swipe the Space bar to the right or left.

Smart typing

Swipe the Space bar from the right or left to switch between languages. With predictive text, you can see suggested phrases and words as you type. You can also add emojis when using this feature. You can also suggest stickers by viewing recommended ones while you're typing. Auto-replace lets you replace the text that you type with those recommendations.

Underline or highlight highlighted words that are incorrectly spelled in red and provide suggestions for corrections. You can also create shortcuts for commonly used phrases. The keyboard's style and layout can be customized.

You can configure the Samsung keyboard to have a higher contrast by increasing its size and changing its colors.

You can customize the keyboard's theme or choose its landscape or portrait mode. Its transparency and size can be adjusted. It also displays special characters and numbers. In addition, you can drag the slider to change the font size.

The settings and services for voice input may be customized. Gestures, feedback, and touch can also be customized. In addition, handwriting options may be customized for Galaxy S23 Ultra only.

Users can write in various text areas and search fields using the stylus known as the S Pen. Its ability to convert handwritten text into written form allows users to edit it with the Galaxy S23 Ultra only.

To save screenshots to the keyboard's clipboard, enable this feature.

You can also enable third-party features and save screenshots directly to the keyboard. You can select which content you want to use and configure the keyboard's features.

Legal and version details for the Samsung keyboard can be found here. You can also contact the company through its members program.

Use Samsung voice input

Instead of typing, speak to enter text with the help of the Samsung keyboard.

CHAPTER SIX

Camera and Gallery

The camera app of Samsung allows users to take high-quality videos and photos. They can be saved to the Gallery, where they can be edited or viewed.

Return to keyboard

Camera

You can enjoy a wide range of professional cameras and video settings. To open the app, tap on the camera icon from the apps that you're using.

Navigate the camera screen

You can easily take stunning photos with your device's rear and front cameras. To start shooting, tap the screen that you want to use the camera to focus on. You can also manually adjust the brightness by dragging the slider.

You can zoom in at a specific angle by pressing 1x and then selecting an option located at the bottom. This is only available with the rear camera.

To change the mode for shooting, 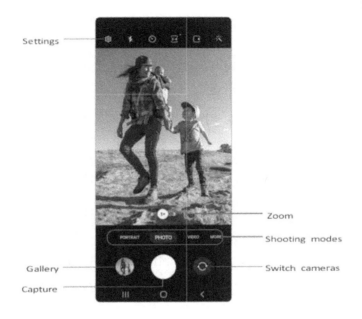 swipe the right or left side of the screen. To change the camera settings, tap on the "Settings" button.

Configure shooting mode

You can configure the camera to automatically identify the appropriate shooting mode for your photos or choose from a variety of other shooting options.

To change the mode for shooting, swipe the right and left sides of the screen. You can also configure the camera to automatically identify the appropriate shooting environment for your photos or choose from a variety of other shooting options.

To add more shooting options to the list, tap on the Add button at the bottom. You can drag the options into the tray located on the right side of the camera screen.

You can download the professional RAW mode and use it to take photos.

While taking pictures, you can manually adjust various settings, such as ISO sensitivity, exposure, and white balance.

In pro videos, you can manually change the ISO sensitivity, white balance, exposure value, and color tone.

One-take photography lets you capture several images and video clips from varying angles.

Multiple photos can be taken from different angles using the single take feature. You can also take pictures in either a vertical or horizontal direction using the Panorama feature.

The director's view allows you to access advanced features, such as the ability to lock onto a subject, swap between different lens settings, and more.

AR Zone

You can easily access all of your augmented reality-based features right from the camera. You can create and customize your own My Emoji character using the tools or the camera.

You can enhance videos with AR Doodle, which adds handwriting or line drawings to your surroundings. It also tracks the movement of objects in your environment.

You can use the camera to create a Deco Pic, which lets you decorate photos and videos in real time. You can also measure items in centimeters or inches using the camera.

Space Zoom

To change the magnification setting, tap on the Zoom shortcut from the camera.

The Galaxy S23 Ultra and other models have a built-in optical image stabilization feature that enables you to take photos with up to a hundred times magnification.

When taking pictures with higher magnification, you can center the subject in the frame and tap on the Zoom lock to use the fastest and most accurate zoom.

Record videos

Smooth videos created using your device will look great.

To change the shooting mode, swipe right or left from the camera. Tap the Record button to start recording. You can also take a picture while you're recording, pause, and resume.

You can enjoy immersive 3D sound with the help of your Bluetooth headphones, which can record 360 audio.

360 audio recording

To enable 360 audio recording, ⬤ go to the camera's settings and choose Advanced video options.

Camera settings

The camera's settings can be customized using the icons found on the main screen or the menu. The options offered by your service provider may vary.

To change the camera's ⬤ settings, go to the main screen or the navigation menu and select the options that are presented.

Intelligent features

You can configure the camera's ⬤ settings by using the icons found on its main screen or the menu. Your service provider may have different options.

You can get expert advice on how to get the perfect shot by using the camera's on-screen guides. You can also scan QR codes with the camera.

Pictures

You can get helpful shot suggestions by using the camera's built-in guides. It can also automatically scan QR codes for added security.

The shutter button is also available to users who want to take a quick burst shot or create an animated GIF with just a swipe to the nearest edge, if desired.

You can add a watermark to your photos' bottom left corner. You can also choose among various file types and save options.

To maximize the utilization of your photos' available space, select the high-efficiency option and save as. Unfortunately, some sharing platforms do not support this format.

In the Pro mode, select which format to save your photos in. You can also save as previews of your selfies. Flipping them aside will not change their appearance.

Brighter videos can be made with the Auto FPS feature, which optimizes the video frame rate automatically.

To maintain focus while the camera is moving, activate the anti-shake feature. You can also enhance your videos with suitable recording resolutions.

To save space, you can record videos in the HEVC format. Unfortunately, some platforms and devices may not support this type of format.

Professional mode allows users to shoot videos at a higher bitrate.

To optimize videos, you can record in the HDR10+ format. Playback devices have to support this standard.

HDR10+ videos are optimized with the help of recording in this format. Playback units must support this type of content.

You can enjoy immersive 3D sound with the help of Bluetooth headphones and 360 audio recording.

The camera's built-in features allow users to track the movement of their subject and keep it in focus. It can also create a viewfinder grid to help with composing videos and pictures.

Press the volume buttons to take photos, record video, and control the volume of the system.

You can also use the camera's 📷 voice commands to take photos. For additional control, you can add a floating shutter button that can be used to take photos anywhere on the screen.

To take a quick snapshot, hold your hand over the camera with your palm facing it.

To change the settings, go to your camera app and select the "Settings" ⚙ option. You can also choose to use the same shooting mode, filter, and selfie angle as the last time.

When taking a picture, 📷 the camera will automatically play a tone. Vibration feedback can also be enabled by tapping on the screen.

You can view the details of Samsung's privacy settings and the various permissions granted to the camera app.

You can reset the camera's settings on other devices. You can also contact Samsung through its members. The camera app and software are also available for viewing.

Gallery

The Gallery app provides a convenient view of the various visual media that your device has. It lets you manage and view your photos and videos.

Tap the Gallery button from the Apps menu.

You can customize the photos and videos that you've stored on your device.

The images presented are for reference only and should not be considered indicative of the current state of affairs with regard to the software and devices.

Pictures

Today

Sort images into custom albums

View pictures and videos

Customize collections of pictures and videos

Pictures Albums Stories

Customize collections of pictures and videos

View pictures

You can view your device's photos in the Gallery app. Tap the picture to view it or swipe to the right or left to view other content. You can also use Bixby Vision to see more information about the picture. Tap the Add to Favorites option to highlight the picture and make it your favorite.

To access the various features, tap the More options. You can view and change the details of the picture, as well as fix the image with automatic enhancements.

Drag the slider to add a portrait effect or reduce the background's visibility in your photos.

Copy the image to a clipboard and paste it into another app. Then, set it as a wallpaper or move it to a secure folder. You can also send the picture to a printer. In addition, you can use the Gallery app's editing tools to enhance your photos.

To start editing a picture, go to the Edit option and select the "Auto adjust" option. This will automatically adjust the image to get the best possible results. You can also flip, twist, crop, or rotate it to change its overall appearance. You can add filters, tone, and exposure effects.

You can add text, stickers, and hand-drawn content to your photos. You can also access the additional features that are available for viewing. Undo the changes that were made to the picture to restore it. Tap the Save option to finish the task. You can also view the videos that are stored on your device, as well as the details of the image.

From the Gallery, tap the pictures button, and then tap the video. Left or right swipes are the ways to view other content.

To add a video to your favorites, tap the Add to favorites button. It will be added to the albums' category under the "favorites" section.

The More options are available to you if you want to access the specific features of the video. You can view and alter the video's details or view it in the default player. You can also set it as a wallpaper or add it to a secure folder.

You can use the following tools to make the most of the video. These include adjusting the audio, changing the volume, and adding background music. You can also trim, rotate, crop, and flip the video to change its overall appearance. In addition, you can add filters to make the video more interesting.

To play the video, tap the Play button. Brightness will enhance the colors in your videos so that they look more vivid and brighter. You can also choose an option to control the brightness of your videos. In the settings, tap Advanced features. You can also manage the videos that you've stored on your gadget.

Brightness, contrast, exposure, and more can be adjusted. Effects, including text, stickers, and photos, can also be added. Reverting the changes made to the video will let you undo them. When prompted, confirm and save.

From the Gallery, tap the pictures button. On the More options page, choose the pictures or videos that you want to share.

After choosing the pictures or videos that you want to share, follow the prompts to select an app or connection to share it with.

Delete pictures and videos

You can remove photos and videos from your device. To do so, go to the Gallery's More options and select the pictures or videos that you want to remove. Confirm and delete when prompted. You can also group related pictures or videos in the Gallery.

You can take a screenshot of your device's screen using the Gallery app. It will then automatically create a gallery album for you.

Release the Volume and Side Down keys from any screen. Then, swipe to take a screenshot.

To take a screenshot of the screen, swipe across the edge from one side to the other to keep it in contact with the device.

To enable this feature , go to the Settings app and select the Advanced features. Then, tap on the Screenshots and Screen Recorder option. You can also modify the settings for taking screenshots. After you've captured a screenshot, the app will show you a toolbar with additional options.

Sharing a screenshot from the toolbar will automatically remove it from your device. Doing so will also delete the screenshots that were taken.

Navigate bars and the status bar should not appear on screenshots. You can also choose whether to save them as PNG or JPG files, and choose a storage location for them.

Write notes, record your device activities, and take a video of yourself using the camera to share with others.

Tap the ▓ Screen Recorder option from the Quick Settings app.

To start recording, choose the sound setting and tap on the Start button.

A countdown will start before the recording begins. Tapping the "Skip" button will immediately start the recording process.

When drawing on the screen, tap the Draw button. You can also use the Pointer to show a shortcut icon on the device when you use your S Pen. You can also take a selfie video with a recording from your device's front camera.

After completing the recording process, tap the "Stop" button to save the recordings to your device's gallery.

Screen recorder settings

You can configure the quality and sound settings for the Screen Recorder.

Go to the Advanced features and select the Screenshots or Screen Recorder option. On the sound setting page, choose the type of sounds that the device will record.

The resolution of the video that you want to record should be set. You can also set the size of the overlay for the selfie video.

Enable the option to show and touch the screen in a recording. You can then save the screen recordings in your device's storage directory.

The list of apps shows the installed and pre-loaded programs. You can also download them from the Google Play store or the Galaxy Store.

To access the list of apps, swipe upward from the Home screen.

Uninstall or disable apps

You can remove installed apps from your device. On the other hand, you can disable or turn off pre-loaded apps.

Tap the "Uninstall/Disable" button from the Apps list. You can also go to the "Search" option if you're not sure where to look for an app or a particular setting.

Go to the Apps list and click on the search button. You'll see matching results for your word or phrase as the settings and apps appear on the screen.

Go to the app that you want to go to by choosing the result. You can customize the settings for the search box by going to the More options and selecting the Customize option. You can also sort the apps by their shortcuts in your custom order or by selecting the ones in the list alphabetically.

Empty icon spaces can be conveniently removed from the list when the apps are arranged manually. They can be done by going to the More options and selecting the Clean up pages option.

Create and use folders

Folders can be created to organize the shortcuts for the apps in the list.

Drag and hold an app shortcut over another until it is highlighted.

The app shortcut should be released to create the folder. Choose the name of the folder, change its color, and add more apps to it. Tap Done to close the folder. You can also copy it to the Home screen.

To add a folder to the list, go to the Apps and tap on the Add to Home button. When you remove a folder, the shortcuts for the apps will return to the list. You can also confirm and delete the process by pressing the "Done" button.

Turn off notifications and optimize your gaming experience to get the most out of your device. To access the navigation bar, go to the bottom of the screen and swipe up from there. There are a few options that are shown on the right and left sides.

To prevent accidental taps, set the screen lock to the default setting.

Performance Monitor and block the navigation bar, as well as block screenshots and screen touches. Game Booster will also configure other options.

App settings

You can manage the installed and pre-loaded apps. From the settings, go to the Apps and select the Customize option.

The default apps will be used when you want to make calls, send messages, browse the web, and more.

You can view and customize the settings of Samsung apps.

To update or view the privacy and usage details of an app, tap it. The options for each app vary.

To reset the settings of apps that have changed, go to More options and select the Reset preferences.

Samsung apps

The following apps may be pre-loaded or downloaded over the air to your device. These can be found in the Google Play Store or the Galaxy Store. The service provider of the device may have different options.

CHAPTER SEVEN

AR Zone

You can easily access all of your AR-related features through the AR Zone app. For more information, please refer to Bixby.

Bixby

Through its personalization technology, Bixby learns about your interactions and suggests content that you might want.

The Bixby app is additionally available for more information.

Galaxy Store

You can find and download premium apps for your Galaxy device that aren't available elsewhere. You'll need a Samsung account to do so.

Galaxy Wearable

You can easily connect your Galaxy Watch to your other device with the help of the app for Galaxy Wearable. You can also get more information about the product by visiting samsung.com.

Game Launcher

The Game Launcher app is designed to automatically organize all of your games. For more information about this feature, please visit the website at Samsung.com/us.

If the Game Launcher is not featured in the list of apps, go to the Settings app and select Advanced features.

You can browse through the gallery and share photos or comment on other people's creations. This community is made up of individuals who use the S Pen to doodle, draw, or paint.

Samsung Free

You can enjoy a wide range of interactive games and live TV shows, as well as articles and news from multiple sources, all for free.

Samsung Global Goals

Through the app, you can also contribute to the Global Goals initiative by making donations to support various causes.

Samsung Members

Through Samsung Members, you can enjoy exclusive content and experiences only available to members, such as support tools and DIY projects. You can get these pre-loaded on your device or through the Google Play Store or Galaxy Store.

Samsung TV Plus

The Samsung TV Plus app offers a variety of free content on mobile and TV devices. Its content includes entertainment, news, and more.

Samsung Wallet

You can easily make payments using your Samsung Wallet, which accepts credit cards in almost any area. You must have a Samsung account to use this feature.

Smart Switch

You can easily transfer photos, contacts, and other files from your old device to another one using the Smart Switch feature.

SmartThings

Through the SmartThings app, you can control and automate various aspects of your home using a mobile device. You can also check the status of your connected gadgets through the dashboard.

The warranty provided by Samsung for connected devices does not cover defects or errors that are not related to the brand. You should contact the manufacturer of the non-Samsung device for assistance.

This page provides a variety of tips and techniques, as well as the operating instructions for your device.

Calculator

The app offers a variety of scientific and basic math functions. It also allows users to convert units.

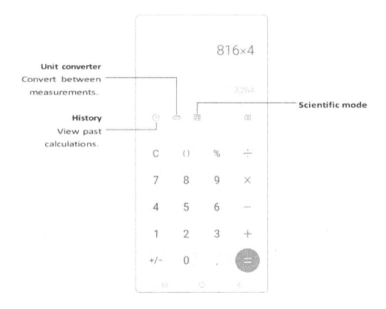

The software and devices are constantly changing, so this page's illustrations are only for reference.

Calendar

The Calendar app can be used to sync and organize all of your appointments across various online accounts.

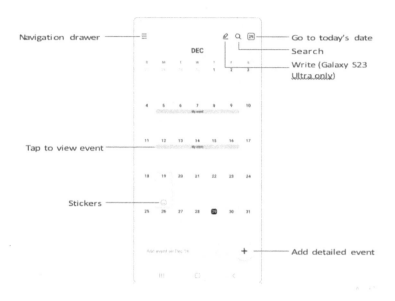

Navigation drawer

Tap to view event

Stickers

Go to today's date

Search

Write (Galaxy S23 Ultra only)

Add detailed event

The software and the devices are constantly evolving, so the illustrations presented here are only for reference.

Add calendars

You can easily add your contacts, email, and other accounts to the calendar app by navigating to the navigation drawer and selecting the type of account that you want to use. You can also set the style of the notifications that appear in the app.

To configure the alert style, go to the Calendar app's navigation drawer and select the option for "Alert style." There are three different options that you can choose from: light, medium, and strong. With the light, you can receive a notification that plays a short sound, while the medium and strong alert rings for a while.

The following alert sounds can be used depending on the style of notification that you want to receive. You can choose between a short or long sound, and the former is for Medium or Light alert tones.

Go to the Calendar app and click on the event that you want to remove. Then, enter the details of the event and select "Save." You can then confirm and delete the event by tapping it again.

Since your device and software are constantly changing, the illustrations presented here should only be used as a reference.

Alarm

You can set recurring or one-time alarms as well as customize the way that they are sent out. To configure an alarm, go to the Alarm tab and select the option for "Time." You can also set the alarm's day and time.

Drag the slider to set the alarm's volume. You can also choose the sound that you want to play for it.

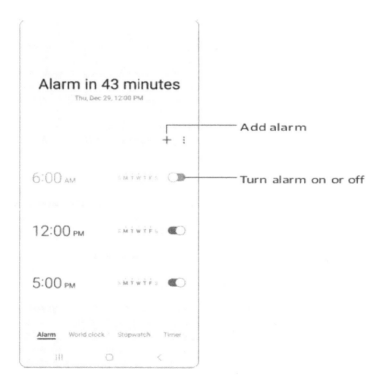

Vibration can be selected as the alarm's mode. You can also set the frequency and duration of the alarm while you snooze. You can then save the alarm.

You can add a bedtime reminder and automatically set your device to sleep mode when it's time for bed. To do so, go to the Sleep option and select the schedule option.

Delete an alarm

You can remove an alarm that you made by pressing the "From Clock" button and holding it. You can also tap the "Delete" option in the alert settings.

You can set your device to vibrate automatically for timers and alarms depending on the Sound mode.

Go to the Settings app and select the option for "Alarm." You can then enable the feature by turning off the system sound. You can also set the number of minutes that you want to be notified before an alarm goes off.

The world clock allows you to keep track of the time in various cities across the globe. You can add or remove cities by dragging the globe, tapping on the desired one, and holding it.

The illustrations presented here are for your reference only, and your device and software will constantly change.

Time zone converter

You can set a time in a specific city within your world clock list to view the local time in the other cities.

From the From Clock app, tap the World clock and select the option for time zone converter. You can then add a new city by pressing the "Add" button.

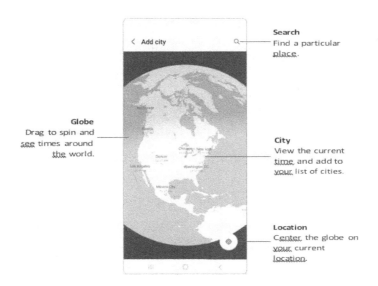

Search
Find a particular place.

Globe
Drag to spin and see times around the world.

City
View the current time and add to your list of cities.

Location
Center the globe on your current location.

You can also set a time by swiping the hours and minutes onto the clock. The time for the other cities will be automatically updated.

To return the clock back to the current time, go to the settings and select the option for Reset. Weather can be enabled or disabled by going to the settings and selecting the option for Show weather. You can also tap Temperature to change it from Fahrenheit to Celsius. The Stopwatch allows you to stop events by a hundredth of a second.

117

To start the timing process, tap the Stopwatch button. To track lap times, tap the Lap button. To stop the clock, tap the Stop to end it. You can then continue timing after the device has stopped working. To reset the stopwatch, tap the Reset option. You can then set a countdown timer for up 99 hours, 59 minutes and 59 seconds.

To set the time, tap the "Timer" button from the menu. You can then use the keypad to set the hours, minutes, and seconds. To stop the timer, tap the Pause button. Tapping Restart will continue the operation. You can then choose the name of the preset timer and save it.

Go to the settings and configure the name and countdown time of the timer you want to save. You can also customize the settings for the feature. You can additionally add your own sound or choose a pre-loaded one.

You can set the timer to vibrate automatically. You can also show a pop-up window when the app is minimized. You can additionally view and configure the other settings for the Clock app.

You can customize the content of supported apps by signing in to your Samsung account.

Through the Samsung Members, you can reach out to the company for assistance. You can also check for the latest software updates and the current version of the Clock app.

CHAPTER EIGHT

Contacts

You can store and manage your contacts on your device. You can also sync with your personal accounts and use calendar and email features.

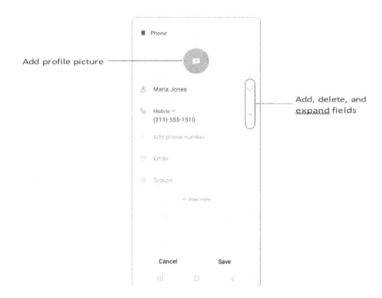

The software and devices are constantly evolving, so the illustrations presented here are only for reference.

Create a contact

To create a contact, go to Contacts and select the option for Create contact. You can then enter the details of the contact and save it.

Edit a contact

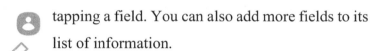

You can change or delete information in a contact by tapping a field. You can also add more fields to its list of information.

Tap Contacts first. From Contacts, select the option to create a new contact. You can then save the details of the contact.

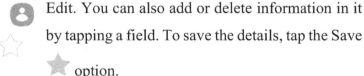

From Contacts, tap the contact and select the option to Edit. You can also add or delete information in it by tapping a field. To save the details, tap the Save option.

When you group contacts into your favorites, they appear at the top of the list and can be easily found within other applications.

From Contacts is where you can tap a contact and select the option to mark it as your favorite. You can also remove it from your Favorites by pressing the Favorites button. You can also share a contact with others using various sharing services and methods. To do so, tap the "Share" option, and then tap either Text or vCard files.

When viewing a contact, tap More > QR code to share the contact information with friends and family. The code updates automatically once the fields are changed.

Show contacts when sharing content

You can share content with your contacts in various applications through the Share window. Upon enabling this feature, your frequent contacts will be shown in the Share window.

To enable the feature, go to the Advanced settings and select Show contacts when content is shared.

You can easily organize your contacts by creating groups. To start a group, go to Contacts and tap the Show navigation menu. You can then select the option to create a group and add information about it. You can also customize its name and ringtone.

To add a new contact, select it from the list and then tap the Done button. You can then choose to add or remove group contacts from the list. From Contacts , go to the navigation menu that's called Groups and tap the option to add or remove groups.

Go to the Edit > Add member section and select the contacts that you want to add. Tap Done to save them.

Send a message to a group

You can send a message to a group by going to the navigation menu that's called Groups and selecting the option to send a message. You can also send an email to a group by going to the Contacts navigation menu and selecting the option to send an email.

Go to the Contacts list and select the contacts that you want to add. Alternatively, you can also tap the All option at the top of the list to choose all.

You can only show group members whose email addresses are in their records. To set up an email account, go to the Contacts menu and select the option to set up an email account. You can then delete a group that you have created.

To only remove the group, tap the group only. Then, remove the contacts and the entire group by pressing the Delete button.

Manage contacts

You can export or import contacts, as well link multiple contacts into a single entry.

By linking multiple entries into a contact, you can consolidate contacts from various sources into one contact.

To manage your contacts, go to the Contacts navigation menu, tap the Show menu, and then select the option to manage contacts.

Merge duplicates of names, email addresses, and phone numbers.

To merge multiple contacts, simply tap the "Merge Contacts" option. The list will then be organized based on the duplicates of names, phone numbers, and email addresses.

Select the contacts that you want to merge and then tap the OK button. You can then import them into your device's virtual card reader. Follow the prompts to complete the process and export contacts.

Go to the Contacts navigation area and select the option that's called Manage contacts. Then, follow the prompts to export or import your contacts. You can then sync all of them into your various accounts. To remove a contact from the list, tap the option to remove a single contact.

Hold and touch a contact to select it, and you can also tap on other contacts to remove them. You can confirm and delete them by pressing the OK button. You can also call emergency contacts even when your device is not connected to the internet. To learn more about this feature, go to the Settings app and select Safety and emergency contacts .

You can add members and choose emergency contacts on your phone. You can also show them on the Lock screen so you can access them immediately in case of an emergency.

CHAPTER NINE

Internet

The Samsung Internet is a fast and reliable web browser that's designed to provide you with a secure browsing experience. It also comes with a variety of features that help protect your privacy and speed up your online surfing.

To learn more about the features of the Samsung Internet, please visit the company's website at samsung.com.

The illustrations presented here are for reference only and do not reflect the current state of the art of devices or software.

Browser tabs

A browser tabs are used to view multiple websites at once. To close a window, go to the Tabs navigation area and then select the Close button. You can create a bookmark to quickly access your favorite sites. You can also add bookmarks to save the webpages that you want to open. Open a bookmark ☆ to launch a new page from the home page.

In the Internet app, 🔵 go to the Tools navigation area and select the Add a page option. There are also various ways to save a page. You can add a page to your bookmark list ☆, view a list of commonly visited sites, or open a page from the home page.

You can create a shortcut for the web page on your home screen and save the content. on your device so you can access it offline. You can also view a list of recent visits to the sites by going to the Tools navigation area and selecting History. Tapping More options will let you clear your browsing history.

You can easily share web pages with your contacts using the Share option in the Internet 🔵 app. Follow the prompts to complete the process.

Secret mode

In Secret mode, webpages are not displayed in your device's search history or browser history. The dark shades of the windows also prevent traces of cookies and other data.

After you close the secret tab, any files that you have downloaded will remain on your device. You can start browsing in secret mode by going to the Tabs navigation area and selecting the Start menu. You can also use biometric or password locks to access the mode. To enable this feature, go to the Tabs navigation area and select the Settings option.

You can restore and remove your data from the secret mode. You can deactivate it and revert to normal browsing by going to Tabs and selecting Turn off Secret mode. You can also change the settings for the apps that you use in the Internet app.

The Messages app lets you send emojis, share photos, and make quick hellos to your contacts. Depending on the service provider, these options may vary.

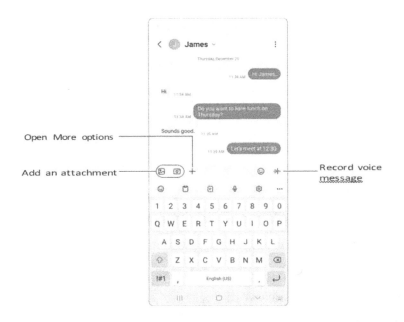

Open More options

Add an attachment

Record voice message

Message search

The Messages app has a feature that lets you search for messages. To use this feature, tap on the search button in the upper-right corner of the app. You can also enter keywords in the search box.

The illustrations presented here are for reference only and do not reflect the current state of the art of software and devices.

Delete conversations

You can remove the conversion history of your contacts by deleting all of their conversations. To do so, go to the Messages app's More options and select the option to "Clear all conversations." You can also send a message with audio or pictures to your contacts in case of an emergency.

To activate the Emergency SOS feature, go to the Settings app and select the Safety and emergency category. You can start the following steps by pressing the Side key multiple times.

You can countdown the seconds before you activate emergency actions. You can also make an emergency call and choose the number to call. You can also share your location with your contacts.

You can also activate the Emergency SOS by pressing both the Volume down and Side keys. Then, pressing the Emergency call.

Emergency sharing

In case of an emergency, send a message with audio or pictures to your contacts.

To set up the Emergency Sharing feature, go to the Settings app and select the Safety and emergency category. You can then choose the type of message that will be sent to your contacts in case of an emergency.

Take and send photos from your rear and front cameras. You can also record audio and send five seconds of it. You can configure the settings for multimedia and text messages.

Emergency alerts

You are not charged to receive an emergency alert, which informs you of imminent danger or other situations.

To customize the notifications sent out for emergency calls, go to the Safety and emergency category and select the Wireless Emergency Alerts option.

You may access emergency notifications in the notifications section of your app. To access the Advanced settings for wireless emergency alerts, go to the settings app's Advanced category.

My Files

You can browse and manage the files that you have on your device, such as music, videos, and images. You can also use the app to access and manage those that are in your cloud accounts.

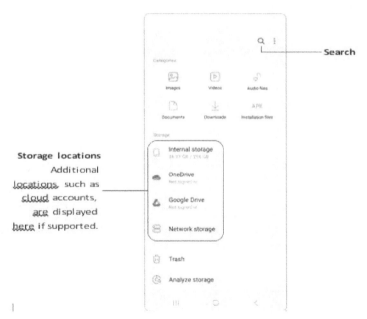

Search

Storage locations
Additional locations such as cloud accounts, are displayed here if supported.

The illustrations presented here are for reference only and do not reflect the current state of the software and devices.

File groups

The groups that are displayed in the device's file system are sorted by the type of file that you have stored. You can view recent files or browse through your collection based on the category that you're in. You can also group related files based on their type.

Your cloud accounts may vary depending on the type of service that you use. You can also check the amount of space that's being used by your files.

My Files settings

Your My Files settings can help you customize the way you manage your files. Depending on the service provider, the options may be different.

To access the settings, go to the My Files app and select the Account option. You can also manage your cloud accounts by connecting to and managing them. You can also customize the way files are displayed and deleted. You can also set a limit on the size of the file that you want to analyze.

CHAPTER TEN

Phone

Aside from making phone calls, the Phone app can also provide various other features. If you have any questions about the app's capabilities, please contact your service provider.

The software and devices are constantly changing, so the illustrations presented here should only be used as a reference.

Calls

The Phone app lets you answer and make calls from the home screen or the Recents tab or Contacts.

Make a call

You can make and answer calls from the home screen using the Phone app. To do so, tap the Call button and enter the number on your device's keypad. You can also tap the Keypad if it's not displayed. The Call log will show all of your calls and all of your missed calls.

Go to Contacts and tap the contact you want to call. Then, swipe across the contact to the right to make the call or answer it.

Answer a call

The name or phone number of the person calling is displayed when the call is received. A pop-up window for the incoming call is shown if you're using an app.

Drag the option "Answer" to the right on the incoming call screen. Alternatively, tap "Answer" to decline the call.

Decline a call

You can decline an incoming call. A pop-up window for the call is shown if you're using an app.

Drag the option Decline to the left on the incoming call screen to reject it and forward it to your voicemail.

Decline with a message

Text messages are also effective ways to decline an incoming call. Drag the message upward and choose it from the drop-down list on the incoming call screen. You can also tap the Send message option to send it or choose it from the pop-up window. You can end a call by pressing the End call button.

You can adjust the volume of the call or switch to a speaker or headset while you're on the phone. You can also use the Volume keys to increase and decrease the call . You can listen to the call through either a Bluetooth headset or a speaker.

You can hear the person calling using either a speaker or a Bluetooth headset.

Multitask

When you're done with the call screen, the status bar will show your active call. You can return to the call screen by dragging the bar down to the Notification panel and pressing the OK button. You can also end the call by pressing the End call option.

You can choose the type of image or video that will be displayed when you receive or make a call. You can also set the layout of the background for the call. For instance, you can show the person's profile picture when they've provided a photo.

When you receive calls while using other apps, these will appear as pop-ups.

To change the way calls are displayed on the phone while using apps, go to Settings > Call display. There are several options that you can choose from.

The Phone app can show an incoming call in its full-screen mode. On the other hand, a small pop-up can be used to show an incoming call at the top of the screen. You can also enable the option to keep the calls in the pop-up window after they've been answered.

You can manage your calls by keeping track of their details in a call log. Among the features you can set are speed dials, voicemail, and blocking numbers. The log also contains the numbers of calls that you have received, missed, or dialed.

To view recent calls 📞 , go to Phone and select Recents. The name of the person who made the call will be shown if they are in your Contacts list.

Save a contact from a recent call

You can use the recent call 📞 data to create a new contact or update your contacts list. To do so, tap Recents from the Phone app.

Go to the call 📇 that you want to save as a contact and click on the Add contacts option.

Go to the contact you want to update or create and select the option to create new contacts.

Delete call records

Go to the contact you want to update or create and select the option to delete call records. To do so, tap on the phone number that you want to block. Then, hold the call that you want to delete and swipe from the log.

Block a number

Placing a call from this number into your Block list will result in it being sent to voicemail and no messages will be received.

To add a contact to the block list , go to Recents, select Details, and then select the option to block contact. You can also confirm your intention by pressing the Block option again.

You can modify the way you block numbers in your settings. From the Phone app, go to the settings section and select the block numbers option.

Speed dial

A contact can be assigned a shortcut number that will allow them to quickly dial their preferred number.

Go to Phone Calls Keypad and select More options for speed dial numbers. The screen will show the reserved numbers.

Unassigned numbers can be selected by pressing the Menu button. Then, choose a different speed dial number from the sequence of calls . Number 1 is reserved for voicemail. You can also type in a name or number and add a contact to the number by pressing the Add from Contacts option. The selected contact will be displayed in the box.

You can make a call with the speed dial option. You can use this feature by holding and touching the number.

First and last digits of the speed dial number should be entered if it is more than one digit long.

Remove a Speed dial number

You can remove an assigned speed dial number by going to the options in the Phone app and selecting the option to remove speed dial numbers. You can also do it by deleting the contact that you want to remove from the dialer.

Emergency calls

Regardless of the service status of your phone, you can still make an emergency call to the designated emergency number in your region.

Go to the emergency number that you want to call and press the "Call" button.

When making an emergency call, you have the opportunity to enjoy various in-call features.

Even if your phone is locked, you can still use it to make an emergency call. The only feature that's accessible to the caller is the emergency calling. The rest of the phone is secure.

Phone settings

You can modify the settings of the Phone app through the phone's settings section. Some calling plans and wireless service providers support different calling services. You can also make a multi-call arrangement while a call is being made.

Depending on the service provider, the options for making and receiving emergency calls may vary. To make a new call, tap the Add call button from the active call. Then, choose the new number and press the "Call." Once the call is answered, switch the numbers and hear the two callers at once using the multi-conferencing feature. You can also make a video call by pressing the "Meet or Video call" button.

Some devices do not support video calling. If they do, the receiver can either accept or reject the call.

Video call effects

In the apps that support video calling, you can customize the background or blur the image of the video call. To enable this feature, go to the Advanced features section and select the option "Video call effects."

You can automatically change the virtual background color to a solid color depending on your environment.

You can also choose an image from your photos to appear as the video call's background. You can make calls over Wi-Fi whenever you are connected to an internet-connected network. To set up and configure this feature, go to the Phone app's settings section and select the option "Wi-Fi calling."

RTT is available whenever you're calling an individual whose phone supports it or a teletypewriter device. The icon for RTT appears on all incoming calls.

RTT calls.

In the settings section, go to the "More options" and select the option "Real time text." You can also configure the appearance of the RTT call button by choosing the option "Visibility." It can be displayed during calls or on the keypad.

To hide RTT keyboard use an external keyboard when connected to an TTY device. You can also select the preferred TTY option for the keyboard.

You can easily track your daily life activities and improve your health with the Samsung Health app. This platform allows you to monitor various aspects of your life, such as your diet and physical activity.

The information collected from this device is not intended to be used in the diagnosis or treatment of any condition or disease.

The data collected by this device and its associated software may be affected by various factors. These include the environment's conditions, your specific activity, the device's settings, and the end-user interactions.

Before you start exercising

Although the app may help you keep track of your activities, it's still important to consult a doctor before starting a new exercise program. According to experts, it's usually safer to start with a moderate exercise program, such as walking, if you have certain health conditions.

Some of the conditions that can be considered are heart disease, diabetes, lung disease, or kidney disease.

Arthritis.

Before you start a new exercise program, make sure that you consult a doctor if you have any symptoms that are suggestive of a serious illness.

Some of the common symptoms of these conditions include pain in the chest, neck, arms, or jaw, as well as loss of consciousness. They can also be accompanied by shortness of breath, dizziness, and swelling in the ankle. A heart murmur or rapid heartbeat is also sometimes a sign of a serious illness.

You must consult a medical professional before exercising, and it is also advisable to speak with your doctor if you are uncertain about your well-being, have a variety of health issues, or are expecting.

Samsung Notes

With the Samsung Notes app, you can easily create and share notes that contain text, images, music, and voice recordings. You can also share your notes through social networking platforms.

To learn more about the features of the Samsung Notes app, please visit the company's website at samsung.com/us.

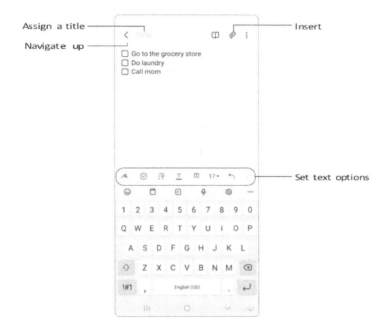

The images presented here are for reference only and should not be considered indicative of the current state of the technology.

Create notes

Compose annotated voice recordings that are perfect for meetings or lectures. You can sync your recordings to the appropriate text and take notes.

Voice recordings

Compose annotated voice recordings for lectures or meetings, and take notes while you're recording audio. Playback allows you to scroll to the relevant text.

Tap the Add button from the Samsung Notes app.

To add content to your recordings, tap the "Add" button from the Samsung Notes app. You can also use the text option to create content while the audio is being recorded. You can also make changes to your notes by selecting "edit" from the list of options . You can manage or sort your notes by clicking on the "manage" button.

You can import PDF files in Samsung Notes. You can also search for a keyword. There are also more options for editing notes, including the ability to share, move, lock, or save as a file. Switch between the different view options, such as "Grid," "List," or "Simple List." You can also pin your favorites to the top of the page, where they will remain.

The Notes menu allows you to view your notes based on their category. To navigate through the various settings, tap the Show navigation menu. You can also view all of your notes by category. You can also view shared notebooks, which are linked to your contacts. You can also trash your notes, which are deleted for up to 15 days after they were last viewed.

Chrome

With Chrome, you can access the Internet using your mobile device and retrieve your bookmarks, address bar, and open tabs from your computer.

Google Drive

Google Drive is a cloud-based storage system that allows you to store and view files. You can also rename, share, and open them. Gmail is a web-based email service that allows you to send and receive emails.

To learn more about Google's offerings, please visit support.google.co.uk/websearch.

Google TV

You can also contact Google's support team for assistance. Google TV is a web-based TV that lets you watch TV shows and movies that have been purchased from the Google Play store. You can also view videos that have been saved on your device.

Maps

You should enable location-based services so that you can get directions and other information from Google Maps.

Google Maps is a web-based app that lets you view and navigate through various areas of the world. You can also make video calls and send and receive messages using the Google app for mobile and tablets.

Google Photos

You can store and backup your photos and videos in your Google Photos account and have them automatically deposited to your Google account. You can also check out new movies, TV shows, books, magazines, and music through the Google Play store.

You can use your Android phone to pay for apps and stores using Google Wallet. You can also watch and upload videos on YouTube right from your device.

YouTube Music lets you stream and browse albums and playlists.

Microsoft apps may be pre-loaded on your device. You can download them from the Google Play or Galaxy Store.

Outlook

You can use Outlook to manage your contacts, calendar, tasks, and email. You can also add an account to the system. To learn more about this and other features, please visit the support page of Microsoft.

These illustrations are only indicative of the current state of the art of software and devices. You should not rely on them to predict the future.

Microsoft 365

You can use the Microsoft 365 app on your device to access Word, Excel, or PowerPoint files. You can also store and backup your files using OneDrive.

OneDrive

You can store and share files, videos, and photos in OneDrive using your phone, tablet, or PC.

Access Settings

You can access your device's ⚙ settings by going to your home screen, choosing the apps that you want to use, and then selecting the settings. Alternatively, you can use the search feature to find the specific setting that you want.

Go to the Connections section and select the option that you want to control.

CHAPTER ELEVEN

Wi-Fi

Without using your mobile data, you can access the Internet using a Wi-Fi network.

Tap the Connections section and choose Wi-Fi and Scan for Existing Networks.

Go to the network and select a password. Then, tap the Connect option to access a hidden network.

Connect to a hidden Wi-Fi network

After scanning the list of networks, you can still access the one that you want by entering the necessary information manually. Before you start, make sure that you have the Wi-Fi network administration's password and name.

To turn on Wi-Fi, go to the Connections section, select the option, and then choose the network that you want to add. You can also enter the information about the network, such as its name, type, and security option.

The password will be entered, and the hidden network will be added. You can also customize other Wi-Fi network-related features, such as the IP and proxy settings.

Scan the QR code using your device's camera to access the Internet.

Wi-Fi Direct

Wi-Fi Direct is a feature that allows users to share data between their various devices. To turn on the feature, go to the settings, and then select the option, and you'll be prompted to connect.

From the Settings app, navigate to the Wi-Fi Direct option, and then choose the device that you want to disconnect.

Intelligent Wi-Fi settings

You can configure your device's connection to different types of hotspots and Wi-Fi networks, view your gadget's network addresses, and manage saved networks. Your service provider may have different options.

Go to the Connections section and choose the Wi-Fi option. Then, select the additional options for intelligent Wi-Fi.

Enable it and your device will automatically switch to mobile data when the connection on your device is unstable. It will also revert to Wi-Fi if the signal is strong.

You can automatically choose to use faster and more stable Wi-Fi connections. You can also turn off Wi-Fi in certain areas when the signal is weak.

The list of available networks displays information such as network speed and stability.

Priority should be given to real-time data, such as video calls and games that are prone to lag.

Suspicious activities may be detected on the network. You'll be notified when this happens.

A power saving mode will let you analyze Wi-Fi traffic to conserve battery. You can also enable automatic hotspot connection when detected. You can view the latest version of the intelligent Wi-Fi option.

Advanced Wi-Fi settings

You can customize the type of networks and hotspots that your device connects to, as well as manage the saved ones. Your service provider's options may vary.

Go to the Connections menu and choose the "Wi-Fi" option. There are also various other options that allow you to customize the settings for your device. You can sync your Samsung Cloud/account Wi-Fi profiles and enable the pop-up that says "Wi-Fi is available" when opening apps.

Wi-Fi and network notifications allow you to receive updates when there are open networks nearby.

You can view and configure saved networks and decide whether to automatically reconnect or disconnect individual ones.

The history of your Wi-Fi usage shows the apps that have turned it on or off recently. You can also connect automatically to supported hotspots and download and install network certificates.

Bluetooth

You can pair your device with other Bluetooth-enabled gadgets, such as a car infotainment system or headphones. When a pairing is made, the devices will remember each other and allow you to exchange data without entering the passkey again.

Follow the steps below to turn on Bluetooth and set up a pair of devices. When you're ready to connect, tap on one of the two devices to use its feature. You can also rename a pair of them to make it easier to identify them.

Unpair from a Bluetooth device

Go to the ⚙ settings and choose "Rename." Then, enter a new name for the device. You can also unpair it from Bluetooth.

To turn on Bluetooth, go to the settings ◗ app and choose "Connections" from the list of options. Then, go to the ⚙ "Settings" category and choose "Advanced."

Advanced Bluetooth settings

Go to the ⚙ settings app and choose Bluetooth Connections 🛜 from the list of options. You can then select the Advanced option for more specific options.

You can sync your files with your Samsung Cloud account and enjoy music streaming through your Bluetooth speakers or headphones.

You can set the ringtone to sync automatically on your device whenever you receive calls from a Bluetooth device. You can also check the apps that have been using Bluetooth recently and block pairing requests.

The Bluetooth scan history app displays the apps that have been detected for Bluetooth devices nearby. It also lets you manage the features of Bluetooth.

Dual audio

You can enjoy dual audio by connecting two Bluetooth devices to each other. To play audio from one device to the other, go to the Notification panel and select Media output. Then, under Audio output, tap next to the devices to play the audio files.

NFC and payment

Tap the Connections tab in the settings app and choose the contactless and NFC payment option.

Tap and pay

An NFC payment app can be used to make a payment by placing your device near a credit card reader. You can turn on NFC and contactless payments by going to the settings app's Connections category and selecting the option "NFC and contactless payments." You can also choose another payment app from the list of available options.

Airplane mode

You can use a payment app that's already open and choose the one that you prefer from the list of options or set it as the default. You can also enable the ability to identify the exact location of nearby devices through ultra-wideband. To access this feature, go to the settings application's Connections section and choose Ultra-wideband.

When activated, Airplane mode disables various network connections, such as mobile data, Bluetooth, calls, and Wi-Fi. While this feature is enabled, you can still turn on Bluetooth and Wi-Fi through the Quick Settings app or the settings app.

To turn on the Airplane mode, go to the settings app and choose the Connections category. Then select the option "Airplane mode."

Mobile devices are subject to local and federal restrictions and guidelines when it comes to onboard use on ships or aircraft. Wi-Fi and ultra-wideband are not allowed onboard vessels or aircraft, and Airplane mode will disable these features. Follow the crew's instructions and check with the appropriate authorities before using your device.

SIM manager

Some wireless service providers allow customers to use a dual SIM card or an eSIM, which is an embedded SIM, for two mobile accounts. The options for this feature vary depending on the service provider.

Some devices with dual SIM support two SIM slots, and they may also come with a microSD expansion slot. After they're released, these devices will receive software upgrades that will enable the capability of dual SIM.

Supports eSIM-equipped devices can be programmed to work alongside the physical SIM card of their mobile device. This enables the use of either the eSIM or physical SIM card for various activities, such as text and voice calls. Upon launch, such devices will be provided with software updates that enable the eSIM feature.

To access the settings app, go to the Connections section and choose the SIM manager. You can view, deactivate, rename, or enable the physical or eSIM cards in your device. You can also add eSIM to a new plan or change the old device's eSIM configuration.

When you have multiple SIM cards, you should set up a primary card for use with texts, calls, and data.

In the Manage your SIM cards section, you can explore the various management options for your cards.

Mobile networks

You can configure your device's reception of mobile network services and its capacity to utilize mobile data. The choices may vary by the service provider.

Tap the Connections tab in the settings app and choose the Mobile networks category. Enable the use of mobile data.

Voice, data, and text roaming settings can be changed for international roaming.

You can configure which networks you can access while roaming. You can also enable the use of data while roaming on other networks.

You can also enable the use of LTE data for enhanced communication. If your service provider provides CDMA roaming, you can change this mode.

The Access Point Names option will allow you to add or choose the APNs that your device will need to connect to its provider.

Choose the network that's right for you. You can also collect usage and diagnostic data for your device. You can additionally check for network extenders, which allow you to extend the connection.

You can check your Wi-Fi and mobile data usage. You can also set different limits and warnings. From the Connections section, tap on the Data usage option.

Turn on Data saver

To conserve your data usage, turn on Data saver. It will prevent certain apps from accessing data in the background.

To turn on the Data saver, navigate to the Connections section, then choose Data usage.

To turn on Data saver, go to the settings app and choose the "Data saver" option. It will prevent apps from accessing the data in the background.

To enable certain applications to utilize the full potential of your device's data, tap the "Allow" option while Data saver is enabled. Then, tap the "Configure" option next to each app to set specific restrictions.

Monitor mobile data

You can set different restrictions and limits for your mobile data usage. The options offered by your service provider may vary.

Tap the Data usage option from the Connections section. There are two types of options for mobile data usage: One is to use mobile data from the plan, and the other is to allow the use of international data roaming.

Setting apps to only use mobile data when connected to the Internet is also a good way to ensure that you don't use excessive amounts of data.

You can monitor your mobile data usage by viewing it over a specific period. You can also see the total amount of data that you have used and the apps that have used it.

You can also change the billing cycle and the data warning schedule to align it with the schedule of your service provider.

These tools can help you keep track of how much data you're using.

Monitor Wi-Fi data

These tools are useful for keeping track of your data usage. You can also customize the networks and limits that you use for Wi-Fi data.

You can view the Wi-Fi data usage that you've used throughout a specific period. In addition, you can see the total app usage.

Mobile hotspot

Using a data plan allows you to establish a private Wi-Fi network for other devices. To turn on the feature, go to the settings app and select Mobile Hotspot.

When prompted, enter the password for your Mobile hotspot. You can connect using your device's Wi-Fi.

The Connected devices category is highlighted under the heading.

Instead of entering a password, you can use a QR code to access the Mobile hotspot by scanning it.

Configure mobile hotspot settings

Using your data plan will allow you to create a secure Wi-Fi network for multiple devices. To turn on Mobile hotspot, go to the settings app, select the category, and then tap on the "Connect" button.

When prompted, enter the password for your Mobile hotspot. You can then connect using your device's Wi-Fi.

The category for "connected" devices is highlighted under the heading.

Scan the QR code to access your Mobile hotspot using another device without entering a password.

You can modify the connection and security settings of your mobile hotspot. From the settings app, go to the Connections section, and then choose the category for Mobile hotspot. You may also change the name of the network.

You can change or view the password that you select for the security level that you want to use. You can also configure the Mobile hotspot's bandwidth options. Lastly, choose the security level that you want to use. You can configure other settings and automatically share your connection with other devices that are linked to your Samsung account.

Go to the settings app, select the category for Mobile hotspot, and then choose the Auto hotspot option. You can then enable the feature by pressing the "enable" button.

Tethering is a type of method that lets you share your mobile hotspot's Internet connection with a different device. The options for this are dependent on the service provider.

In the Connections section, go to the menu item that says "Mobile hotspot and tethering. " Then choose the option that allows you to share your Bluetooth connection with another device. You can also connect a computer to the gadget through a USB cable.

Nearby device scanning

You can easily set up a connection to other devices with the help of Nearby, which will notify you whenever there are available connections.

Go to the Connections section and select More settings and Nearby scanning. Then turn on the feature and connect to a printer.

Connect to a printer

You can easily print photos and documents from your device using a printer that's connected to the same network.

To add a printer, go to the settings page and select More options under the Printing section.

If the printer requires a plugin, follow the steps below to add a print service.

Some apps do not support printing.

Virtual Private Networks

A VPN is a type of secure network that allows you to connect to it from your device. You'll need to provide the connection details to use it.

In the Connections section, go to the menu item that says "Virtual Private Networks" and then choose the option that allows you to add a VPN profile. You'll need to enter the network information that your network administrator provides. You can then manage your VPN connection.

After you've set up a VPN, go to the settings page and select the option that says "Manage VPN." You can then choose to remove or update the VPN. To connect to a VPN, go to the Connections section and select the option that allows you to add a VPN profile. You'll need to enter the network information that your network administrator provides.

Ethernet

Tap the VPN and then choose Disconnect. You can configure your gadget to use a private DNS host to access the internet. In the settings section, select More options and Private DNS. Then, go to the section where you want to configure the connection.

An Ethernet cable can be used to connect your device to the local network if the wireless connection is unavailable.

To use an Ethernet cable, go to the settings page and select More options and follow the prompts. Make sure that you have an Ethernet adapter, as it is required to connect the cable to your device.

The status of your device's network lock and whether it can be used on another network will be displayed. The options for using another network may vary depending on the service provider.

Tap the Connections menu item and then choose More options and the Network lock status.

Connected devices

You can configure your device to achieve mobile continuity and allow other connected gadgets to work seamlessly together. You can also customize the settings for your gadget to allow anyone with a Samsung ID to share files with it.

When you make a call or answer a call, Galaxy Buds will automatically switch to this device.

You can make and answer calls and send text messages from other Galaxy devices that are linked to your Samsung account.

You can also continue using apps on other Galaxy devices that are connected to your Samsung account.

You can easily access your contacts, messages, and photos using Windows computers and devices.

You can also use the keyboard and cursor to control the device from your Galaxy Book.

The DeX feature allows you to connect your Galaxy device to a TV or a computer for enhanced multitasking capabilities.

The DeX feature also allows you to connect your Galaxy device to a TV or a computer for enhanced multitasking capabilities. You can use the Smart View feature to show and play videos on a nearby TV.

You can use Android Auto to connect your device to compatible car displays so you can focus on driving.

CHAPTER TWELVE

Sounds and vibration

The vibrations and sounds that your device makes to signify notifications and other interactions can be controlled.

Sound mode

You can set your device to vibrate while ringing and use it for notifications only. You can also set it to mute and prevent sounds.

You can modify the sound mode of your device without the volume buttons by going to the settings page and selecting Sounds and Vibration.

You can use the volume levels, sounds, and vibrations that you have set in your Sound preferences to get notifications and alerts.

Instead of using the volume buttons to set the sound mode, you can set it manually. This will allow you to customize the sound levels without losing them.

Instead of using the volume buttons to set the sound mode, you can use the sound mode setting. This will allow you to customize the sound levels without losing them.

Mute with gestures

Turn the device around or cover the screen to quickly mute sounds.

In the settings page, go to the Advanced features section and select Motions and gestures. Then, tap on the Enable button to activate the vibration feature.

You can set the frequency and duration of the vibrations that your device makes. You can customize the sounds that it makes for calls and notifications by going to the settings page and selecting Sounds and Vibration. You can also configure the intensity of the vibration by dragging the slider.

Some of the gestures that you can use to vibrate your device are: holding the navigation buttons and swiping across the screen. You can also use the phone keypad to make and answer calls. On the keyboard, you can vibrate when using the Samsung keyboard. You can also use gestures to charge your device.

Drag the sliders to configure the intensity of the vibration for different touch interactions, notifications, and calls.

Volume

The volume level for various sounds can be customized, such as calls, media, notifications, and system sounds. You can drag the sliders for each of these sound types to configure the volume level.

The Volume keys can be used to adjust the volume of your device. When pressed, the pop-up menu will show the current sound type and the volume level. Expanding the menu will let you change the volume of the other sounds by dragging their sliders.

Use Volume keys for media

The default setting will turn on the volume control for media sounds and not for any particular sound type.

To enable the vibration feature, go to the settings page, select Sounds and vibration, and then choose the Use Volume keys for the media.

Media volume limit

Enables limiting the maximum audio output of your device while using headphones or Bluetooth speakers that aren't included.

To enable this feature, go to the settings page, select Sounds and vibration, and then choose the Media volume limit. Drag the slider for the Custom volume limit option. You can also change the volume setting by pressing the Set volume limit PIN.

Ringtone

You can customize your ringtone by adding your own or choosing from a variety of preset sounds. The options offered by your service provider may vary.

Go to the settings page and select Sounds and vibration. You can also customize the ringtone by adding your own or choosing from a variety of preset sounds. On the notification sound page, choose a preset that will play all of the notifications that you receive.

Drag the slider to change the volume of the notification sound. Then, tap on the preview to hear it and choose it.

Notifications sounds can be customized for specific apps through the settings menu.

System sound

You can personalize the sounds 🔊 of your device for certain actions, such as charging or tapping the screen. The settings offered by your service provider may vary.

Go to the Settings app and select Sounds and vibration and then choose System sound. Drag the slider to change the volume of the system sound.

A system sound theme can be used to play various sounds for touch interactions and other activities. It can also be customized to change the mode and volume for different functions.

Different sounds can be used for different touch interactions, such as tapping or touching the screen. They can also be used for calling and typing on the Phone keypad. Keyboards, such as the Samsung Galaxy S24, allow users to use sound when typing on the device. When a charger is connected, sounds play when the screen is locked or unlocked.

Dolby Atmos

When playing content that's been specifically mixed for Dolby Atmos, you can enjoy the best possible audio experience. This feature only works with a headset connected to the device.

To configure the sound quality and effects, go to the Sounds and vibration section of the Settings app and choose Sound quality.

Go to the settings app and select Sounds and vibration. You can configure the sound quality and effects for Dolby Atmos. It offers a deeper and more immersive audio experience with its ability to flow around and above you.

Equalizer

You can manually change the audio settings or select an audio preset that's customized for different genres of music.

To configure the effects and sound quality, select the Sounds and vibration option from the menu. Then, choose the music genre that you want to hear.

UHQ upscaler

This enables enhanced audio clarity for videos and music. This only works with a headset that is connected.

Go to the Sounds and vibration section of the Settings app and choose Sound quality. You can also customize the sound quality and effects for each ear. To change the settings, go to the Adapt sound option and select when to switch.

Go to the settings app and select the sound profile that you want to use. Then, tap on the Customize option to customize the sound quality and effects.

Separate app sound

A separate app sound can be played on a Bluetooth headset or speaker without the other sounds, such as notifications. To enable this feature, you must connect a Bluetooth device to the app.

To enable the feature, go to the Settings app and select the separate app sound option. Then, turn on the option to enable the feature. You can also choose which audio device you want to play the app's sound on.

Notifications

You can prioritize the notifications sent by different apps by changing the way they notify you.

App notifications

Select which apps are permitted to send notifications.

Tap on the option to enable individual notifications from the Notifications section of the Settings app.

Lock screen notifications

You can set which notifications are shown on the lock screen.

To enable the feature, go to the Notifications section of the Settings app and select Lock screen notifications. You can also customize the notifications that you receive.

To hide notifications, go to the Notifications section of the Settings app and select Lock screen notifications. You can then show or hide the content of the notifications by choosing which ones to show on the lock screen.

184

You can modify the style and other settings for the notifications you receive. From the settings app, tap on the Notification pop-up option and select Brief. This allows you to customize the way notifications are shown.

You can choose the type of edge lighting that you want for your notifications. You can additionally customize the colors for those that contain specific keywords.

You can show notifications even while the screen is off.

The default Samsung settings are enabled for notifications.

CHAPTER THIRTEEN

Do not disturb

Turning on the do not disturb mode allows you to block notifications and sounds while the screen is off. You can also set a time for recurring events such as meetings or sleep.

Go to the settings app and select Notifications. You can then configure the settings for the do not disturb mode. You can set a specific duration for the mode and also customize the time for recurring events.

You can create a new schedule for your device and set the days and times when you will put it in the do not disturb mode.

Allowed during Do not disturb

Enable the Do not Disturb exceptions for calls and messages.

You can add apps that you want to receive notifications in the Do not Disturb mode. Even if you do not allow the associated apps to send messages, calls, and conversations, they will still reach you.

You can also enable the sounds and vibrations for various notifications, such as alarms and events, while the do not disturb feature is active.

You can customize the appearance and content of notifications by going to the Settings app and selecting Advanced settings. You can also configure the notifications that are sent by apps and services. You can additionally show the number of notifications that are displayed on the Status bar and the battery percentage.

You can view and set priority for conversations by holding and touching the notification. You can also set it as silent or alert.

You can enable the ability to display floating notifications in the Smart pop-up or Bubbles view.

The notifications app provides a suggestion system that lets you identify the appropriate actions to take in response to messages and notifications.

You can also enable the ability to show a button that lets you snooze your notifications.

Enable or customize the notifications sent by certain services and apps and set recurring reminders for them. Clear them to stop the notifications.

On the left-hand side of the notification app, you can see which apps have active badges that show the number of unread messages.

You can customize the notifications that are sent by apps and services for emergency alerts.

Alert when phone picked up

You can set your device to notify you whenever there's been a missed call or message by vibrating it whenever you pick it up.

To enable the feature, go to the Settings app and select Advanced features. Then, select Alert when phone is picked up.

Display

You can also customize the font size, brightness, and timeout settings.

Dark mode

Dark mode turns your device's screen into a dark and relaxing environment, which reduces the brightness of your notifications and white or vibrant screens.

To change the color theme of your device, go to the settings app and select the "Display" option. You can also customize the settings for the Dark mode.

You can configure the Dark mode to automatically turn on whenever there's a sunrise or sunset.

Screen brightness

You can configure the Dark mode for either the Custom schedule or Sunset to sunrise. You can also adjust the screen brightness based on your personal preference. In the Display section, you can drag a slider to set a custom level.

To set the screen brightness ⚙ automatically according to the lighting conditions, go to the Adaptive Brightness option.

Tap the Extra option to boost the screen's brightness if Adaptive Brightness is disabled. This will use more battery.

The Quick settings panel can also be used to change the brightness ⚙ of the screen.

Motion smoothness

You can change the brightness of your device from the Quick Settings panel. Motion smoothens ⚙ scrolling and makes animations more realistic by increasing the refresh rate.

Eye comfort shield

This feature can help reduce eye strain and improve your sleep quality. You can set a schedule so that it will automatically turn on and off.

Go to the Settings app, tap the Display option, and then select the Eye comfort shield. You can also configure the option to customize its appearance.

The Adaptive Brightness feature will adjust the screen's color temperature according to your preferred usage patterns and the day of the week.

You can set the schedule for when the eye comfort shield should be turned on. On the schedule, select "Always on," "Sunset to sunrise," or "Custom." Drag the slider to set the filter's opacity. This feature provides enhanced comfort by adjusting the display's contrast and color tones.

Screen mode

The device has various screen mode options that can adjust the quality of the screen depending on the situation.

In the settings app, go to the Display section, and then select the option for Screen mode. Drag the slider to set the white balance and then click Advanced to manually change the values of the RGB. You can also customize the style and font size of the device's font.

You can select a font or ✚ download the Galaxy Store's fonts to add to your device. You can also change the font's size and make it appear with bold weight. To make content easier to view, adjust the screen zoom.

Screen resolution

The resolution of the device's screen can be lowered to conserve battery life or increase it to enhance the image quality.

To change the resolution ⚙ of your device's screen, go to the Settings app and select the option for Screen resolution.

Some applications may not support higher- or lower-screen resolution settings. When you change the resolution, these may stop working.

Full screen apps

You can select the apps that you want to use with the full-screen aspect ratio.

Go to the Settings app and select the option for Full screen applications. You can configure the feature and customize the apps that support it.

Camera cutout

A black bar can hide the camera cutout.

Tap the Display option from the Settings app and select the camera cutout and customize the apps that support it.

Screen timeout

You can set a specific amount of time that the screen will turn off. To set a time limit for the screen timeout, go to the Settings app and select the option for Display.

Unnecessary prolonged exposure to non-moving images may result in degraded image quality or a ghost-like effect. To avoid this, turn off the display screen completely when not in use.

Accidental touch protection

Turn off the screen's ability to detect touch input when the device is in dark conditions, such as a bag or pocket.

To activate the feature, go to the Settings app, and then select the option that allows you to enable accidental touch protection. You can also enable the feature by going to the Display section and selecting Touch sensitivity.

Show charging information

The estimated battery level and time until the device fully charges will be shown when the display is off.

To enable the charging feature, go to the Display option and select the option for Show charging.

Screen saver

You can view photos in a photo table or a photo frame. You can also view photos from your Google account by going to the Photos app and selecting the option for

Photos. To start a demonstration of the Screen saver, tap the option next to the feature that you want to use. You can also use the Lift to wake feature to turn on the device and activate its display.

Go to the Settings app and select the option that allows you to enable the Lift to wake feature. This feature will automatically wake up the device and activate the display.

Double tap to turn on screen

Instead of using the Side key, double-tapping the screen will turn it on.

To enable the gesture and motion feature, go to your device's settings app and select the Advanced features option.

Double tap to turn off screen

You can turn off the device's display using the double tap method instead of the Side key.

Go to the settings app and select Advanced features and scroll down to the Motion and Gesture option.

Keep screen on while viewing

You can use the front camera to keep the device's screen turned on while you're looking at it.

To turn on the motion and gesture feature, go to the Advanced features section and select the option for Keep screen on while you're viewing.

One-handed mode

You can modify the layout of the device's display to make it easier to operate it with one hand. To enable the feature, go to Settings, Advanced features, and select the option for One-handed mode.

To decrease the device's display size, tap the home button twice in succession. You can also set a screen lock to protect your data and secure your device.

Google apps

Google apps are available for pre-installed on your device. You can download these apps from the Google Play store.

Screen lock types

There are various types of screen lock options that you can choose from, such as high, medium, and no security.

Biometric locks can also be used to protect sensitive information on your device. See Biometric security.

Set a secure screen lock

You should always use a screen lock that is secure to protect your device. To enable biometric locks, you must first set up and configure them.

To set a screen lock, go to the 🔒 Settings app and select Screen lock type. ⬛ You can then choose the pattern and password that you want to use.

To set the lock screen to show notifications, tap the option that says Show content. You can also hide notifications from the Notification panel or show content only when the screen is opened.

You can set the type of notifications that will appear on the lock screen and show on the Always On Display option. To exit the menu, tap Done.

A screen lock is necessary for the Smart Lock feature, which will automatically unlock your device whenever a trusted location is detected.

You can customize the settings for your device's secure lock. You need a screen lock for this feature.

You can change the appearance and customize the items featured on the lock screen. You can also modify the widget that appears with the clock.

You can choose whether to allow certain items to be edited by holding and touching them on the lock screen.

The Always On Display option is enabled, and this provides additional information about this feature.

The time when you're at home and where you are while you're roaming will be displayed on the Roaming clock.

The Roaming clock shows the time when you are at home or in the middle of a roaming adventure. It also displays the current location of both you and your device.

Find My Mobile

Through the use of Find My Mobile, you can keep your device secure and track its online location to prevent it from being stolen or lost. It can also delete your data remotely. To use this feature, you must have a Samsung account and turn on Google's location service.

Turn on Find My Mobile

Before you can use the feature, you must first turn it on and configure the options. You can also access it remotely through the website findmymobile.samsung.com.

In the Privacy and Security section, select the option to allow this phone to be found.

You can access the feature through your Samsung account by going to the settings app and selecting the option that says Enable Find My Mobile.

Enable this option to allow this feature to find your device.

Samsung can store your device's PIN, password, or pattern for remote access. This feature enables users to control their device from anywhere.

When the battery level drops below a certain threshold, your device can send its last known location to the website of Find My Mobile.